Nelson Mathematics 3

Teacher's Resource

Chapter 10: Division

Series Authors and Senior Consultants
Marian Small • Mary Lou Kestell

Senior Authors
Heather Kelleher • Kathy Kubota-Zarivnij • Pat Milot
Betty Morris • Doug Super

Teacher's Resource Chapter Author
Carole Adam

Assessment Consultant
Damian Cooper

THOMSON
★
NELSON

Australia   Canada   Mexico   Singapore   Spain   United Kingdom   United States

THOMSON

NELSON

**Nelson Mathematics 3
Teacher's Resource**

**Series Authors and
Senior Consultants**
Marian Small, Mary Lou Kestell

Senior Authors
Heather Kelleher,
Kathy Kubota-Zarivnij, Pat Milot,
Betty Morris, Doug Super

Authors
Carole Adam, Anne Cirillo,
Jennifer Brown, Jack Hope,
Wendy Klassen, Joanne Languay,
Marian Small, Ian Stackhouse,
Susan Stuart, Stella Tossell

Assessment Consultant
Damian Cooper

Director of Publishing
David Steele

Publisher, Mathematics
Beverley Buxton

Senior Program Manager
Shirley Barrett

**Teacher's Resource
Program Managers**
Alan Simpson
David Spiegel

Developmental Editors
Janice Barr
Julie Bedford
Jenna Dunlop
Anna Garnham
James Gladstone
Adrienne Mason
Margaret McClintock
Janice Nixon
Frances Purslow
Elizabeth Salomons
Tom Shields
Alan Simpson
Michael Tabor

Editorial Assistant
Megan Robinson

**Executive Managing Editor,
Development & Testing**
Cheryl Turner

**Executive Managing Editor,
Production**
Nicola Balfour

Senior Production Editor
Linh Vu

Copy Editor
Linda Szostak

Senior Production Coordinator
Sharon Latta Paterson

Production Coordinator
Franca Mandarino

Creative Director
Angela Cluer

Art Director
Ken Phipps

Art Management
ArtPlus Ltd., Suzanne Peden

Illustrators
ArtPlus Ltd.

Interior and Cover Design
Suzanne Peden

Cover Image
T. Kitchin/First Light

**ArtPlus Ltd. Production
Coordinator**
Dana Lloyd

Composition
Valerie Bateman/ArtPlus Ltd.

**Photo Research and
Permissions**
Vicki Gould

Printer
Frisby Litho

**National Library of Canada
Cataloguing in Publication**

Nelson mathematics 3.
Teacher's resource / Marian Small ...
[et al.].

ISBN 0-17-620094-0

1. Mathematics—Study and
teaching (Primary)
I. Small, Marian
II. Title: Nelson mathematics three.

QA135.6.N443 2003 Suppl. 3
510   C2003-904834-9

Contents

OVERVIEW

Introduction 1
Curriculum Across Grades 2 to 4: Division 2
Math Background: Research and Important Issues 3
Planning for Instruction 3
Problem Solving 3
    Connections to Literature 3
    Connections to Other Math Strands 3
    Connections to Other Curricula 3
    Connections to Home and Community 3
    Chapter 10 Planning Chart 4
Planning for Assessment 6
    Chapter 10 Assessment Chart 7
Reading Strategies 8

TEACHING NOTES

Chapter Opener 9
Getting Started: Sharing Tickets 10
Lesson 1: Sharing to Divide 13
Lesson 2: Grouping to Divide 17
Lesson 3: Communicate About Division 21
Mid-Chapter Review 25
Math Game: Fill-a-Row Division 28
Lesson 4: Exploring Division Patterns 29
Mental Math: Using Equal Groups 32
Lesson 5: Estimating Quotients 33
Lesson 6: Division Strategies 37
Skills Bank 41
Problem Bank 43
Chapter Review 44
Chapter Task 47

CHAPTER 10 BLACKLINE MASTERS

Family Newsletter 49
Chapter 10 Mental Math 50
Chapter 10 Test 52

Chapter 10 Task 54
Scaffolding for Getting Started Activity 56
Scaffolding for Do You Remember? 57
Scaffolding for Lesson 2 59
Scaffolding for Lesson 5 60
Scaffolding for Lesson 6 61
Beginning Division Strips 62
Mixed Division Strips 63
Number Cards 64
Answers (Problem of the Week, Mental Math,
    Chapter Test, Chapter Task, & Scaffolding) 65
From Masters Booklet
    Initial Assessment Summary (Tool 1) 1
    What to Look for When Assessing Student
        Achievement (Tool 2) 2
    Coaching Students Toward Success (Tool 3) 3
    Conducting In-Class Student Interviews 4
    Student Interview Form (with prompts) (Tool 4) 5
    Student Interview Form (without prompts) (Tool 5) . . 6
    Problem-Solving Rubric (Tool 6) 7
    Understanding of Concepts Rubric (Tool 7) 8
    Application of Mathematical Procedures
        Rubric (Tool 8) 9
    Communication Rubric (Tool 9) 10
    Using the Assessment of Learning Summary—
        Individual Student 11
    Assessment of Learning Summary—Individual
        Student (Tool 10) 12
    Using the Assessment of Learning Summary—
        Class by Strand 13
    Assessment of Learning Summary—Class by
        Strand (Tool 11) 14
    Using the Assessment of Learning Skills Chart 15
    Assessment of Learning Skills Chart (Tool 12) 16
    100 Chart 31
    10-by-10 Grid 33
    Number Lines 34

Introduction

This chapter extends students' work in division from Grade 2 in which

- division is seen only as a way to divide objects into equal groups
- students used concrete materials as their main method of dividing

This chapter also prepares students for work in Chapter 12, Fractions, in which the use of division is required for calculating fractions of sets and mixed fractions.

Strategy Focus: Problem Solving
Lesson 4 helps students use their division skills to identify, describe, and extend patterns involving division.

Curriculum Across Grades 2 to 4: Division

All the Grade 3 expectations listed below are covered in this chapter.
When the expectation is a focus of a particular lesson, the lesson number is indicated in brackets.

Grade 2	Grade 3	Grade 4
Overall Expectations: • understand and explain basic operations (addition, subtraction, multiplication, and division) of whole numbers by modelling and discussing a variety of problem situations	**Overall Expectations:** • understand and explain basic operations (division) involving whole numbers by modelling and discussing a variety of problem situations **(1, 2, 3)** • develop proficiency in multiplying and dividing 1-digit whole numbers **(1, 2, 4, 5, 6)** • select and perform computation techniques appropriate to specific problems and determine whether the results are reasonable **(1, 2, 5)** • solve problems and describe and explain the variety of strategies used **(3, 5, 6)**	**Overall Expectations:** • select and perform computation techniques appropriate to specific problems involving whole numbers and decimals, and determine whether the results are reasonable • solve problems involving whole numbers and decimals, and describe and explain the variety of strategies used • justify in oral or written expression the method chosen for calculations beyond the proficiency expectations for pencil-and-paper operations: estimation, mental computation, concrete materials, algorithms (rules for calculations), or calculators
• use a calculator to solve problems beyond the required paper-and-pencil skills	• use a calculator to solve problems beyond the required pencil-and-paper skills **(6)**	
Specific Expectations: **Computations** • demonstrate division as sharing • use one fact to find another	**Specific Expectations:** **Computations** • use a calculator to examine number relationships and the effect of repeated operations on numbers **(2, 6)** • interpret division sentences in a variety of ways **(1, 2, 3)** • identify numbers that are divisible by 2, 5, or 10 **(4)** • demonstrate and recall division facts to 49 ÷ 7 using concrete materials **(1, 2, 4, 5, 6)**	**Specific Expectations:** **Computations** • relate division to multiplication • multiply and divide numbers using concrete materials, drawings, and symbols (see proficiency expectations) • interpret multiplication and division problems using concrete materials, drawings, and symbols • recall multiplication and division facts to 81
Applications • use a calculator to solve problems with numbers larger than 50 in real-life situations • pose and solve number problems with at least one operation	**Applications** • use appropriate strategies to solve number problems involving whole numbers **(1, 2, 4, 5, 6)** • use various estimation strategies to solve problems, and then check results for reasonableness **(5)** • identify relationships between subtraction, multiplication, and division **(1, 2, 4, 6)** **Understanding Number** • count backward by 2s and 5s **(4)**	**Applications** • select the appropriate operation and solve one-step problems involving whole numbers and decimals with and without a calculator • pose problems involving whole numbers and solve them using the appropriate calculation method: pencil and paper, calculator, or computer • explain their thinking when solving problems involving whole numbers • recognize situations in problem solving that call for multiplication and division, and interpret the answer correctly

Math Background: Research and Important Issues

Word Meanings for Division: At this early stage of learning about division, students can sometimes confuse division with subtraction because of the complexity of the relationship between the two. The connection between multiplication and addition is relatively simple. For example, $3 \times 2 = 6$ or $2 + 2 + 2 = 6$ shows 3 groups of 2. Multiplication and division are also easy to connect, especially in the use of fact families. For example, $3 \times 4 = 12$; therefore, $12 \div 4 = 3$. The connection between division and subtraction is not as simple or apparent to students. For example, $6 \div 2 = 3$ shows 6 divided into 2 groups, giving 3 in each group. Subtracting $6 - 2 - 2 - 2 = 0$ shows that you need 3 groups of 2 repeatedly subtracted from 6.

Recall of Facts: Students who clearly understand the concept of division may begin to make the change from counting objects (or using a number chart) to locating answers, to memorizing their division facts to $49 \div 7$. The key areas of this chapter allow students to

- get a solid grasp of the concept of division
- have opportunities to discuss and solve related problems
- make a connection between multiplication and division and subtraction and division

Although recall of division facts is beneficial and useful as students get older, rote recall with no understanding of the concept of division is not encouraged unless students have specific learning needs that make understanding difficult.

Using Manipulatives: Since the numbers used in most lessons are reasonably low, the use of counters, a number line, or a 100 chart is suggested. The use of a calculator is required in Lesson 6, Division Strategies.

Planning for Instruction

Problem Solving

- Assign a Problem of the Week each week from the selection below or from your own collection.
  1. There are 24 students who want to play soccer. There must be 6 students on each team. How many teams can be made?
  2. How can you find out if 6 children can share 44 tickets equally? Explain your answer. Use a model.

Connections to Literature

Add books to your classroom that are related to the math in this chapter. For example:

Divide and Ride (Stuart J. Murphy; HarperCollins Children's Books, 1997)

The Doorbell Rang (Pat Hutchins; Morrow, William & Co., 1992)

Fair Bear Share (Stuart J. Murphy; HarperCollins Publishers, 1997)

Great Divide: A Mathematical Marathon (Dayle Ann Dodds; Candlewick Press, 1999)

One Hundred Hungry Ants (Elinor J. Pinczes; Houghton Mifflin Company, 1999)

One Hungry Cat (Joanne Rocklin; Scholastic, Inc., 1997)

A Remainder of One (Elinor J. Pinczes; Houghton Mifflin Company, 2002)

Connections to Other Math Strands

Measurement: Students may relate division directly to daily applications such as reading or following instructions for a recipe (as seen on the chapter cover page).

Patterns and Algebra: Students have many opportunities to look for counting patterns and relationships between division and multiplication or division and subtraction. They can use concrete objects to model their solutions.

Data Management: Students may use their knowledge of tallies, charts, and graphs to display results of further research connected to Lesson 6 or to the Chapter Task.

Connections to Other Curricula

Science: Experimentation is an important part of the Grade 3 science curriculum, especially in the area of plant studies. Students can use division when calculating quantities involved in science experiments.

Health and Physical Education: In Lesson 2, students can apply the concept of division in Question 5 to dance in the gym. Dividing students into groups for various kinds of teams, dances, or other activities will show a real application of this concept.

Social Studies: In Lesson 6, students connect division with the height of the CN Tower. Students can research other large buildings in Canada's urban communities and compare heights using charts or graphs.

Connections to Home and Community

- Invite a parent or community worker to share ways in which division is used on the job.
- Send home the Family Newsletter (Master on p. 49).
- Have students complete the *Math 3 Workbook* pages for this chapter at home.
- Use the At Home suggestions found in most lessons.

Chapter 10 Planning Chart

Key Ideas

Benchmark numbers are useful for estimating and comparing numbers.
Multiplication and division are extensions of addition and subtraction.
Multiplication and division are intrinsically related.
There are many algorithms for performing a given operation.
Patterns underlie mathematical concepts and can also be found in the real world.

Chapter Goals

Explain division in a variety of ways.
Use strategies to solve division problems.
Relate division to multiplication.

Student Book Section	Lesson Goal	ON Expectation	Pacing 10 days	Prerequisite Skills/Concepts
Getting Started: Sharing Tickets, pp. 238–239 (TR pp. 10–12)	Use concepts and skills developed prior to this chapter.		1 day	• Understand and explore basic multiplication. • Skip count backward. • Explore patterns and pattern rules.
Lesson 1: Guided Activity Sharing to Divide, pp. 240–241 (TR pp. 13–16)	Use words and symbols to describe division by sharing.	3m4, 3m6, 3m23, 3m27, 3m88	1 day	• Skip count backward by 2s, 3s, 4s, and 5s. • Subtract repetitive numbers from a larger number. • Divide objects into equal groups.
Lesson 2: Guided Activity Grouping to Divide, pp. 242–243 (TR pp. 17–20)	Divide by counting equal groups.	3m4, 3m6, 3m23, 3m27, 3m88	1 day	• Skip count by 2s to 7s. • Use a number line. • Divide by sharing.
Lesson 3: Guided Activity Communicate About Division, pp. 244–245 (TR pp. 21–24)	Use a model to explain how to divide.	3m4, 3m8, 3m23	1 day	• Use counters and number lines to skip count backward by 2s, 5s, and 10s. • Divide by sharing and grouping. • Explore division problems (sharing) using concrete materials.
Lesson 4: Exploration Exploring Division Patterns, p. 248 (TR pp. 29–31)	Identify, describe, and extend division patterns.	3m6, 3m14, 3m24, 3m27, 3m32, 3m88	1 day	• Skip count forward and backward by 2s, 3s, 4s, 5s, 6s, 7s, and 10s. • Identify number patterns used in counting.
Lesson 5: Direct Instruction Estimating Quotients, pp. 250–251 (TR pp. 33–36)	Solve division problems using estimation.	3m6, 3m7, 3m8, 3m27, 3m32, 3m33	1 day	• Divide by sharing and grouping up to 49 ÷ 7. • Skip count by 2s, 5s, and 10s. • Solve problems using pictures, words, and numbers.
Lesson 6: Direct Instruction Division Strategies, pp. 252–253 (TR pp. 37–40)	Use estimation and multiplication to solve division problems with greater numbers.	3m6, 3m8, 3m10, 3m22, 3m27, 3m32, 3m88	1 day	• Skip count backward by a variety of numbers. • Estimate using multiplication and division. • Use a calculator.
Mid-Chapter Review: p. 246 (TR pp. 25–27) **Math Game:** p. 247 (TR p. 28) **Mental Math:** p. 249 (TR p. 32) **Skills Bank:** pp. 254–255 (TR pp. 41–42) **Problem Bank:** p. 256 (TR p. 43) **Chapter Review:** p. 257 (TR p. 44–46) **Chapter Task:** p. 258 (TR p. 47–48)			3 days	

Materials	Masters/Workbook	Extra Practice and Extension in the Student Book
counters 15/student (optional) student-made multiplication table, 1/student	(for Extra Support) 100 Chart, Masters Booklet p. 31 (for Extra Support) Scaffolding p. 56 (for Extra Support) Scaffolding p. 57	
counters (optional) paper plates and tickets student-made multiplication table, 1/student	(for Extra Support) Number Lines, Masters Booklet p. 34 (for Extra Support) 100 Chart, Masters Booklet p. 31 Workbook p. 77	Mid-Chapter Review Questions 1 & 3 Skills Bank Questions 1–3
counters (optional) calculator	(for Extra Support) Number Lines, Masters Booklet p. 34 (for Extra Support) 100 Chart, Masters Booklet p. 31 (for Extra Support of Questions 5–8) Scaffolding p. 59 Workbook p. 78	Mid-Chapter Review Question 2 Skills Bank Questions 5–7 Chapter Review Questions 2 & 3
counters	(for Extra Support) Number Lines, Masters Booklet p. 34 (for Extra Support) 100 Chart, Masters Booklet p. 31 Workbook p. 79	Mid-Chapter Review Question 6 Skills Bank Questions 9, 10, 11, 13, & 14
pencil crayons large number line for the floor	(for Extra Support) Number Lines, Masters Booklet p. 34 (for Extra Support) 100 Chart, Masters Booklet p. 31 Workbook p. 80	Mental Math Student Book p. 249 Skills Bank Questions 9–11 Chapter Review Question 9
play coins (loonies) counters	(for Extra Support) Number Lines, Masters Booklet p. 34 (for Extra Support) 100 Chart, Masters Booklet p. 31 (for Extra Support of Questions 5–7) Scaffolding p. 60 Workbook p. 81	Skills Bank Question 12 Problem Bank Questions 2, 5, & 7 Chapter Review Question 10
calculators	(for Extra Support of Questions 5–9) Scaffolding p. 61 Workbook p. 82	Skills Bank Questions 13 & 14 Problem Bank Question 8
	Chapter 10 Test Pages 1 & 2, pp. 52–53 Chapter 10 Task Pages 1 & 2, pp. 54–55 Workbook p. 83	

Planning for Assessment

The Chapter 10 Assessment Chart on the next page lists many opportunities for assessment using a variety of strategies: written questions, interview, short answer, investigation, observation, and product marking. To guide you, refer to the recording tools and samples provided in the Masters Booklet pages 1 to 16.

Managing Initial Assessment

- To see the specific assessment suggestions for Getting Started, refer to pages 10 to 12 in this booklet. This initial assessment opportunity includes the exploratory activity, Sharing Tickets, and a four-part skills-based question in Do You Remember?
- You may use other initial assessments involving informal interview or written questions (for example, your own diagnostic activity).
- Use Initial Assessment Summary (Tool 1) to help you record your observations and concerns about the prior knowledge that an individual brings to Chapter 10. You may choose to record observations for all students, or for only those individuals who appear to be having difficulty.

Managing Assessment for Feedback

- To see the specific assessment suggestions for Lessons 1 to 6, refer to the second column of the Chapter 10 Assessment Chart on the next page.
- You may use other informal feedback assessments involving ongoing observations and interviews to help you adapt your instruction to suit the needs of individual students.
- Use any of these tools to help you improve student achievement:
  What to Look for When Assessing Student Achievement (Tool 2)
  Coaching Students Toward Success (Tool 3)
  Student Interview Form (with prompts) (Tool 4)
  Student Interview Form (without prompts) (Tool 5)
- **Peer Assessment:** As students are working together, encourage them to listen to one another and learn from each other.
- **Self Assessment:** As students are working through the chapter, encourage them to practise at home. They can use the Skills Bank or the Workbook.
- **Journal Writing:** Good opportunities for journal writing occur in the Reflecting or the Consolidation section in any lesson.

Managing Assessment of Learning

- Refer to the last four columns of the Chapter 10 Assessment Chart on the next page. There you will find detailed support for all the Key Assessment Questions in Lessons 1 to 6, and all the questions in the Mid-Chapter Review and Chapter Review, as well as the Chapter Task. Which of these opportunities you choose to assess will depend on the quantity of evidence you need to gather for individual students.

  Note: When charts show levels of student achievement, they are always based on the appropriate parts of the four generic rubrics (scoring scales):
  Problem-Solving Rubric (Tool 6)
  Understanding of Concepts Rubric (Tool 7)
  Application of Mathematical Procedures Rubric (Tool 8)
  Communication Rubric (Tool 9)
- If you want to assess other questions from the lessons, the Problem Bank, or the Problems of the Week, use the appropriate rows from the four generic rubrics to create your own question-specific rubric.
- Use any of these tools to help you record and track student achievement:
  Using the Assessment of Learning Summary— Individual Student
  Assessment of Learning Summary—Individual Student (Tool 10)
  Using the Assessment of Learning Summary—Class by Strand
  Assessment of Learning Summary—Class by Strand (Tool 11)
- **Self Assessment:** After students have completed the chapter, encourage them to try Test Yourself on Workbook page 83. (Answers to these multiple-choice and all other Workbook questions can be found at **www.mathk8.nelson.com**.)
- **Journal Writing:** A good opportunity for journal writing occurs in the Chapter Review. One prompt students might use is "The most important things to do when dividing are…"

Managing Chapter Evaluation

- Look at the assessment data you've recorded throughout the chapter on Tools 10 and 11. Also include any end-of-chapter information from either the Chapter 10 Test Pages 1 & 2, pp. 52–53 or the Chapter 10 Task Pages 1 & 2, pp. 54–55. Determine the most consistent level for an individual.

Chapter 10 Assessment Chart

Student Book Lesson	Assessment for Feedback Chart	Assessment of Learning			
		Chart	Question/Category	ON Expectations	Strategy
Lesson 1: Guided Activity Sharing to Divide, pp. 240–241	TR p. 13	TR p. 16	5, Understanding of Concepts	3m4, 3m6	written question
Lesson 2: Guided Activity Grouping to Divide, pp. 242–243	TR p. 17	TR p. 20	6, Understanding of Concepts	3m4, 3m6	short answer
Lesson 3: Guided Activity Communicate About Division, pp. 244–245	TR p. 21	TR p. 24	4, Communication	3m4, 3m8	written question
Mid-Chapter Review, p. 246		TR p. 26–27	1, Understanding of Concepts	3m4, 3m6	written question
			2, Understanding of Concepts	3m4, 3m6	written question
			3, Understanding of Concepts	3m4, 3m6	written question
			4, Communication	3m4	written question
			5, Application of Procedures	3m6	short answer
			6, Problem Solving, Communication	3m8	written question
Lesson 4: Exploration Exploring Division Patterns, p. 248	TR p. 29	TR p. 31	entire exploration, Problem Solving	3m14, 3m21	investigation
Lesson 5: Direct Instruction Estimating Quotients, pp. 250–251	TR p. 33	TR p. 36	7, Understanding of Concepts	3m7, 3m8	written question
Lesson 6: Direct Instruction Division Strategies, pp. 252–253	TR p. 37	TR p. 40	6, Problem Solving	3m8, 3m12, 3m22	written question
Chapter Review, p. 257	TR pp. 45–46		1, Understanding of Concepts	3m4, 3m6	short answer
			2, Communication	3m4	written question
			3, Understanding of Concepts	3m4, 3m6	short answer
			4, Communication	3m4, 3m6	written question
			5, Understanding of Concepts	3m4, 3m6	short answer
			6, Understanding of Concepts	3m4, 3m6	short answer
			7, Communication	3m4	written question
			8, Communication	3m8	written question
			9, Problem Solving	3m21	written question
			10, Problem Solving	3m33	written question
			11, Application of Procedures	3m27	short answer
Chapter Task, p. 258	TR p. 48		entire task, Problem Solving	3m4, 3m7, 3m27, 3m32	observation and product marking

Reading Strategies

Reading for Understanding	Strategies
Getting Started **Noting details in pictures and illustrations:** By looking carefully at the illustration, students will have a better understanding of the problem.	• Ask students to describe what is happening in the picture. • Ask them how many tickets you need to feed the animals and how many tickets you need to ride the Zoomobile. • Ask how noting the details in pictures/illustrations can help them to solve the problem.
Lesson 1 **Building a mathematical vocabulary:** By clarifying the meaning of the words *division* and *quotient*, students will have a better understanding of the operation of division.	• Have students explain what happens when you share. • Tell them that in mathematics, division is a way to share. • Ask if anyone knows what the result of division (or sharing) is called. If no one knows the answer, provide the word *quotient* for students. • Ask why it helps to know multiplication facts when you divide.
Lesson 2 **Comparing plans:** By comparing two different plans for the same problem, students will have a better understanding of the concept.	• Have students look at Sharleen's and Amit's plans, and explain how they are alike and how they are different. • Ask students why there might be more than one way to solve math problems.
Lesson 3 **Communicating mathematically:** By reading Michael's Explanation, students will understand the importance of clear, complete, and organized communications.	• Ask students to explain why it is important to communicate using math language. • Ask how Michael could use the Communication Checklist to improve his explanation. • Ask if there is anything in Michael's explanation that they would change.
Mid-Chapter Review **Identifying key words and symbols:** By identifying key words in a question, students will better understand how to respond to the question.	• Ask students to identify the words that tell them what they need to do to answer the questions (e.g., model, show, write, divide, etc.). • Ask how identifying key words will help them to respond appropriately to the questions.
Math Game **Reading and following procedures to play the Math Game:** By reading through the steps, students will understand how to play Fill-a-Row Division	• Ask students to identify what materials they will need to play the game. • Ask how many people can play this game. • Ask them to explain the game in their own words.
Lesson 4 **Reading the problem closely and carefully:** By reading each section of the problem closely and carefully, students will have a clear understanding of what they are being asked to do.	• Ask students to identify the key words in prompts A to F (extend, colour, describe, etc.) • Ask how identifying the key words will help them to complete the problem.
Lesson 5 **Using the title to make predictions:** By reading the title of this lesson, students will predict the task to follow.	• Ask students to remember the meaning of the terms *estimate* and *quotient*. • Ask them to check the meaning by reading the definition of these words in the glossary. • Ask them to read the title to identify what they will be doing in this chapter.
Lesson 6 **Reviewing the example:** By carefully reviewing the example, students will have a better understanding of estimation and multiplication as division strategies.	• Ask students to explain, in their own words, how Brady solves the problem. • Ask them to describe the procedures used to divide using multiplication and using estimation.
Skills Bank/Problem Bank/Chapter Review **Finding key information and following directions:** By selecting the key information in a problem and following directions, students will find the information they need to help solve the problems and answer the questions.	• Ask students what they can do to find the key information in the questions in the Skills Bank and the problems in the Problem Bank and Chapter Review (e.g., read the questions/problems carefully, identify key words, look at diagrams, etc.).
Chapter Task **Reading a recipe:** By reading a recipe, students will have a better understanding of how measurement works in a real-life situation.	• Ask students what kind of information they get from reading the recipe (ingredients, amount of juice needed, kind of juice, etc.). • Ask why it is important to read and follow a recipe exactly as written.

Chapter Opener

Using the Chapter Opener

Introduce this chapter by discussing the photograph on Student Book page 237, which shows students following written instructions to make a recipe for punch. Students should read and discuss why the use of numbers in the recipe is important. Ask questions such as the following:

- What numbers are used in the recipe? (three number 8s and 24)
- What is the connection between the three number 8s and the number 24? (3 groups of 8 or $3 \times 8 = 24$)

Have a brief discussion about the goals of this chapter. Ask students for examples of multiplying. Discuss what is meant by the word "strategy" and where students have already used strategies in their math work.

After discussing the goals of the chapter, have students brainstorm ideas about how multiplication and division are used in everyday life. Ask them to look through the chapter for examples. Be sure to introduce the idea of using a recipe, which is the focus of the Chapter Task on Student Book page 258.

Ask students to record in their journals their thoughts about one of the goals, using a prompt such as "The ways that multiplying and dividing are related are…" At the end of the chapter, you can ask students to complete the same prompt and compare their responses, and reflect on what they have learned.

At this time, it would be appropriate to

- send home the Family Newsletter
- ask students to look through the chapter and add math word cards to your classroom word wall. Here are some terms related to this chapter:

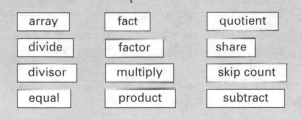

array	fact	quotient
divide	factor	share
divisor	multiply	skip count
equal	product	subtract

Division

CHAPTER 10

Goals

You will be able to

- explain division in a variety of ways
- use strategies to solve division problems
- relate division to multiplication

PUNCH
makes 24 cups
8 cups gingerale
8 cups grape juice
8 cups apple juice
Mix well. Chill and serve.

Sharing punch

Family Newsletter Master, p. 49

Getting Started: Sharing Tickets

Grade 2 Skills/Concepts

- Understand and explore basic multiplication.
- Skip count backward.
- Explore patterns and pattern rules.

Use these pages as an opportunity for initial assessment and to give you a sense of students' understanding and recall of multiplication facts from Grade 3 and division from Grade 2, as well as their experience with number patterns. Observe what students can do and what they're having difficulty with. Record your notes using the Initial Assessment Summary for each individual.

Preparation and Planning

Pacing	**25–35 min** Activity **15–25 min** Do You Remember?
Materials	• counters 15/student • (optional) student-made multiplication table, 1/student
Masters	• (for Extra Support) 100 Chart, Masters Booklet p. 31 • (for Extra Support) Scaffolding p. 56 • (for Extra Support) Scaffolding p. 57 • (for Assessment) Initial Assessment Summary, Masters Booklet p. 1
Vocabulary/ Symbols	skip count, pattern, pattern rule, share, divide, multiply, product

Using the Activity (Pairs) ◗ 25–35 min

Ask students if they have ever been to a zoo. Ask them, "What types of activities and things can you find at a zoo?" Possible responses include various rides, zoo exhibits, food and drink, money, and tickets. Refer students to the picture on Student Book page 238.

Keenan and his friends have bought some tickets at the zoo. Ask students, "If you were to go to a zoo with friends, what kinds of things might you share?" Provide each student or pair of students with a set of at least 15 counters to represent things they might share. For those students who might have difficulty, provide copies of **Scaffolding Master p. 56**.

Most students can use counters to respond to prompts A to D. Work through prompts A and B together, and then allow students time to respond to prompts C and D on their own. When they are finished, discuss their strategies and answers.

If time allows, other counting patterns can be added to the discussion. For example:

Prompt A "If only 2 people wanted to share 12 tickets, how would that change the answer?" Explain or draw a model for the answer.

Prompt C "What if Karla needed 18 or 21 cones, how many tickets would she need now?" Explain or draw a model for the answer.

Prompt D "If Krista wanted to take a friend on the rides with her, how many tickets would they require altogether?" Explain or draw a model for the answer. This question involves doubling, which connects well with multiplication and number patterns.

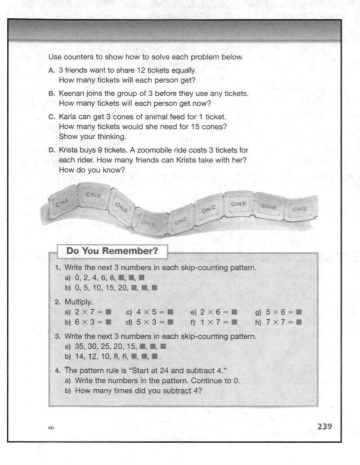

Use counters to show how to solve each problem below.

A. 3 friends want to share 12 tickets equally. How many tickets will each person get?

B. Keenan joins the group of 3 before they use any tickets. How many tickets will each person get now?

C. Karla can get 3 cones of animal feed for 1 ticket. How many tickets would she need for 15 cones? Show your thinking.

D. Krista buys 9 tickets. A zoomobile ride costs 3 tickets for each rider. How many friends can Krista take with her? How do you know?

Do You Remember?

1. Write the next 3 numbers in each skip-counting pattern.
   a) 0, 2, 4, 6, 8, ■, ■, ■
   b) 0, 5, 10, 15, 20, ■, ■, ■

2. Multiply.
   a) 2 × 7 = ■   c) 4 × 5 = ■   e) 2 × 6 = ■   g) 5 × 6 = ■
   b) 6 × 3 = ■   d) 5 × 3 = ■   f) 1 × 7 = ■   h) 7 × 7 = ■

3. Write the next 3 numbers in each skip-counting pattern.
   a) 35, 30, 25, 20, 15, ■, ■, ■
   b) 14, 12, 10, 8, 6, ■, ■, ■

4. The pattern rule is "Start at 24 and subtract 4."
   a) Write the numbers in the pattern. Continue to 0.
   b) How many times did you subtract 4?

NEL   239

Using Do You Remember?
(Individual) ▶ 15–25 min

Observe students to see whether they can answer the questions correctly. If Extra Support is required, guide those students and provide copies of **Scaffolding Master p. 57**.

Lesson 6 of Chapter 9, on pages 230 to 231 of the Student Book, involves making a multiplication table. Students may benefit from using their own student-made multiplication tables to find both multiplication facts and skip-counting answers. When using the multiplication table, place one index finger on a factor at the top of the multiplication table and the other index finger on the other factor along the side of the table. Move the fingers toward each other. The fingers will meet at the product.

Answers

A. 4 tickets

B. 3 tickets

C. 5 tickets (3 × 5 = 15 cones)

D. 2 friends

1. a) 10, 12, 14
   b) 25, 30, 35

2. a) 14
   b) 18
   c) 20
   d) 15
   e) 12
   f) 7
   g) 30
   h) 49

3. a) 10, 5, 0
   b) 4, 2, 0

4. a) 24, 20, 16, 12, 8, 4, 0
   b) 6

Division as equal sharing and repeated subtraction	When Students Have an Area of Strength	When Students Have an Area of Need
• Prompt A (Understanding of Concepts)	• Students use counters to model division as sharing (partitioning).	• Students may make mistakes in modelling sharing. Have students draw three circles to represent three friends, and then act out the sharing (one-for-you, one-for-you method).
• Prompt B (Understanding of Concepts)	• Students adjust the model created in prompt A to create a model of a new division question.	• Students may continue to share the counters in three groups. Ask students to state how many friends there are now. Have students draw a new circle to represent the change.
• Prompt C (Understanding of Concepts)	• Students use counters to create sets of three to find the number of sets (measurement/repeated subtraction model of division).	• Students may continue to use one-by-one sharing. Model taking out equal groups of three from the total.
• Prompt D (Understanding of Concepts)	• Students describe division in terms of equal groups.	• Students may not include Krista in the final count. Ask students to say how many altogether can ride, and then how many friends she can take.

Do You Remember?	When Students Have an Area of Strength	When Students Have an Area of Need
• Question 1 (Application of Procedures)	• Students skip count by 2s and 5s to correctly complete a number pattern.	• Students may need to refer to a number line or a 100 chart to accurately continue the pattern.
• Question 2 (Application of Procedures)	• Students recall multiplication facts to 7×7.	• Some students will benefit from the continued use of counters to find correct products. Review multiplication thinking strategies learned in Chapter 9.
• Question 3 (Application of Procedures)	• Students skip count backward by 2s and 5s to correctly complete a number pattern.	• Students may skip count forward rather than backward. Have students describe the number pattern in words before extending it.
• Question 4 (Understanding of Concepts)	• Students use a given rule to accurately create a pattern and identify the number of decreases.	• Students might count the number of terms in the pattern rather than the number of times the pattern changes. Have them draw an arc below the terms to indicate each backward jump of four.

Extra Support:
Scaffolding Master p. 56

Extra Support: 100 Chart,
Masters Booklet p. 31

Extra Support:
Scaffolding
Master p. 57

Assessment: Initial
Assessment Summary,
Masters Booklet p. 1

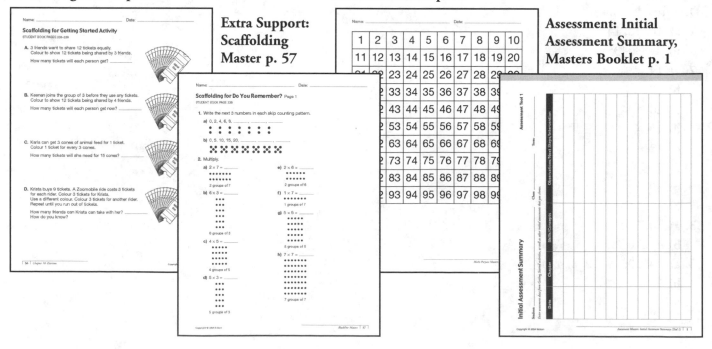

Sharing to Divide

 Goal Use words and symbols to describe division by sharing.

Prerequisite Skills/Concepts

- Skip count backward by 2s, 3s, 4s, and 5s.
- Subtract repetitive numbers from a larger number.
- Divide objects into equal groups.

Expectations

3m4 understand and explain basic operations ([addition, subtraction, multiplication,] division) involving whole numbers by modelling and discussing a variety of problem situations

3m6 develop proficiency in multiplying and dividing one-digit whole numbers

3m23 interpret [multiplication and] division sentences in a variety of ways

3m27 demonstrate and recall [multiplication facts to 7×7 and] division facts to $49 \div 7$ using concrete materials

3m88 identify relationships between [addition,] subtraction, multiplication, and division

Assessment for Feedback	What You Will See Students Doing...	
Students will	**When Students Understand**	**If Students Misunderstand**
• share objects equally among groups	• Use counters and draw models, identifying total numbers and group numbers accurately.	• Students might draw the correct total number of objects, but not in the correct groupings. Provide plates or circles on paper for them to organize the groups.
• write a division sentence that shows the model	• Write the division sentence using the correct numbers, in the correct order (e.g., $6 \div 3 = 2$).	• Students may use the correct numbers, but say or write them in the wrong place (e.g., $3 \div 6 = 2$). Remind students of the language related to dividing. The total divided by the number of groups is the number in each group. For example, say, "6 counters shared in 3 groups is 2 in each group." Relate this language to the number sentence.

Preparation and Planning

Pacing	**10–15 min** Introduction **20–30 min** Teaching and Learning **10–15 min** Consolidation
Materials	• counters • (optional) paper plates and tickets • (optional) calculator • student-made multiplication table, 1/student
Masters	• (for Extra Support) 100 Chart, Masters Booklet p. 31 • (for Extra Support) Number Lines, Masters Booklet p. 34
Workbook	p. 77
Vocabulary/ Symbols	sharing, divide, quotient
Key Assessment of Learning Question	Question 5, Understanding of Concepts

Meeting Individual Needs

Extra Challenge

- Students can make a list of school activities in which sharing is required (such as dividing students into teams) and calculate different answers.

Extra Support

- Additional practice in skip counting using number lines or 100 charts is always helpful. Some students may benefit from using the repeat function key of a calculator to skip count.

  `2 + = = = =`

- Students who require additional practice using the sharing strategy to divide may benefit from using 100 charts, counters, or student-made multiplication tables.

Introduction (Whole Class)
♦ 10–15 min

Have three students stand at the front of the class. Demonstrate how to share objects fairly among them (e.g., 6 pencils, 9 erasers, 12 pennies, etc.). Ask students how they know each person will get the same number of objects. If possible, at some point, provide a new sharing situation and turn the demonstration over to several students.

This would be an excellent time to read *The Doorbell Rang* and act out the sharing.

Teaching and Learning
(Whole Class) ♦ 20–30 min

Read and discuss Charlie's Sharing on Student Book page 240. Ask students to respond to prompt A using all of their counters. Work through prompt B together and write the division sentence that would match the sharing model. Discuss the vocabulary words *division* and *quotient*.

Reflecting

In this section, students answer three summary questions. Here the relationship between multiplication and division begins to emerge. Discuss each question, encouraging students to refer to their responses to prompts A and B.

Consolidation ♦ 10–15 min
Checking (Pairs)

For intervention strategies, refer to Meeting Individual Needs and the Assessment for Feedback chart.

4. Encourage students to use counters to model the answer. After they complete parts a) and b), have the class model their answers and discuss part c) together.

Practising (Individual)

6. & 7. Remind students that modelling includes pictures, words, and number sentences in each answer. Encourage students to use number lines, multiplication charts, or counters to assist with calculating the answers.

Closing (Whole Class)

Have students summarize the meaning of vocabulary words, such as *division* and *quotient*, and explain the connection between sharing and division. Review Reflecting Questions 1 and 2.

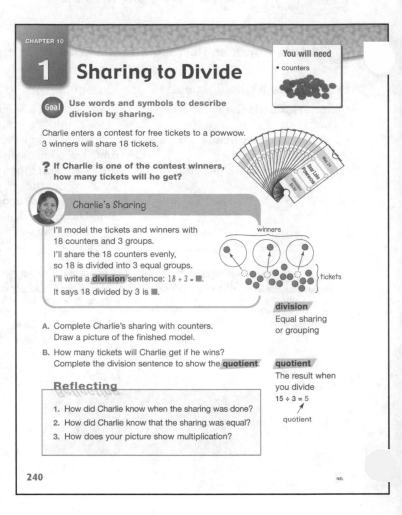

Answers

A.

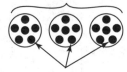

B. 6 tickets; $18 \div 3 = 6$

1. For example, Charlie knew the sharing was done when he ran out of counters to share.
2. For example, he knew the sharing was equal because each plate had the same number of counters.
3. For example, $3 \times 6 = 18$ (3 groups of 6 make 18).
4. **a)** 4; for example:

b) $8 \div 2 = 4$
c) For example, the division sentence means 8 tickets shared by 2 people is 4 tickets each.

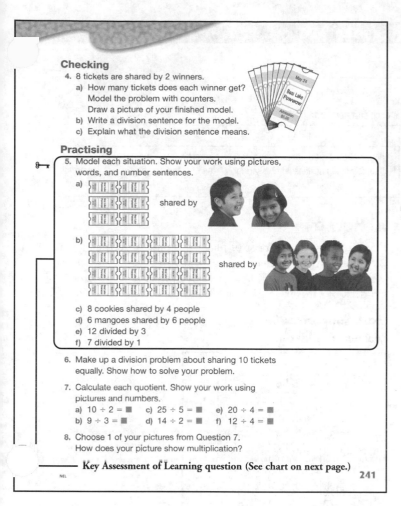

Checking

4. 8 tickets are shared by 2 winners.
   a) How many tickets does each winner get?
      Model the problem with counters.
      Draw a picture of your finished model.
   b) Write a division sentence for the model.
   c) Explain what the division sentence means.

Practising

5. Model each situation. Show your work using pictures,
   words, and number sentences.
   a)

   shared by

   b)

   shared by

   c) 8 cookies shared by 4 people
   d) 6 mangoes shared by 6 people
   e) 12 divided by 3
   f) 7 divided by 1

6. Make up a division problem about sharing 10 tickets
   equally. Show how to solve your problem.

7. Calculate each quotient. Show your work using
   pictures and numbers.
   a) $10 \div 2 = \blacksquare$ c) $25 \div 5 = \blacksquare$ e) $20 \div 4 = \blacksquare$
   b) $9 \div 3 = \blacksquare$ d) $14 \div 2 = \blacksquare$ f) $12 \div 4 = \blacksquare$

8. Choose 1 of your pictures from Question 7.
   How does your picture show multiplication?

—— **Key Assessment of Learning question** (See chart on next page.)

NEL
241

---

c) For example:

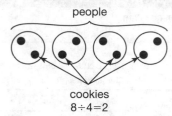

people

cookies
$8 \div 4 = 2$

8 cookies shared by 4 people is 2 cookies each.

d) For example:

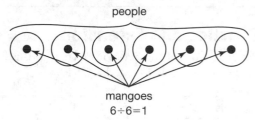

people

mangoes
$6 \div 6 = 1$

6 mangoes shared by 6 people is 1 mango each.

e) For example:

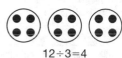

$12 \div 3 = 4$

12 shared by 3 groups is 4 each.

f) For example:

$12 \div 1 = 12$

12 shared by 1 group is 12.

6. For example: "If 10 tickets are shared by 5 people, how
   many tickets does each person get?"

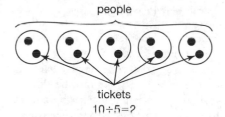

people

tickets
$10 \div 5 = 2$

10 tickets shared by 5 people is 2 tickets each.

7. a) 5   b) 3   c) 5
   d) 7   e) 5   f) 3

8. For example, in part e), my picture shows 4 groups of 5;
   $4 \times 5 = 20$.

---

5. a) For example:

students

tickets
$6 \div 2 = 3$

6 tickets shared by 2 people is 3 tickets each.

b) For example:

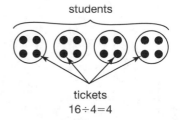

students

tickets
$16 \div 4 = 4$

16 tickets shared by 4 people is 4 tickets each.

Assessment Strategy: written question
Understanding of Concepts

Question 5
- Model each situation. Show your work using pictures, words, and number sentences.
  (Score 1 point for each correct model [pictures, words, and number sentences] for each part, for a total of 6.)

1	2	3	4
• demonstrates an inaccurate understanding of division by sharing	• demonstrates a growing but still incomplete understanding of division by sharing	• demonstrates grade-appropriate understanding of division by sharing	• demonstrates in-depth understanding of division by sharing

Extra Practice and Extension

- You might assign any of the questions related to this lesson, which are cross-referenced in the chart below.

Mid-Chapter Review	Student Book p. 246, Questions 1 & 3
Skills Bank	Student Book p. 254–255, Questions 1–3
Problem Bank	Student Book p. 256, Question 1
Chapter Review	Student Book p. 257, Questions 1 & 2
Workbook	p. 77, all questions
Nelson Web Site	Visit **www.mathk8.nelson.com** and follow the links to *Nelson Mathematics 3*, Chapter 10.

Math Background

Dividing through sharing means taking a group of objects and sharing them equally among a specific number of people or groups. Dividing a package of 12 muffins among 6 friends is an example of sharing. Sharing is an important concept to understand at the beginning of division. A total number of objects divided into a specific number of groups tells you the number in each group.

Remember to have students use manipulatives and number lines all through this chapter. It is useful for them to have many chances of success with appropriate tools, after which they will be ready to let go of concrete materials. Always speak about the use of thinking tools like number lines and counters positively. If you tell student to use these tools only if they need to, students may give them up before they are ready.

Common Misconception: Some students may confuse the divisor with the dividend when writing the question. It is important to establish the correct order at the beginning of this chapter. Remind students that the larger number that tells about the whole group before it is divided must come first, just as the whole group exists before it is broken up into smaller groups.

At Home

- Students can make a list of places at home or in the community where sharing is required (e.g., dividing up the money when playing a game of Monopoly or sharing a deck of cards for a game).

Extra Support: 100 Chart, Masters Booklet p. 31

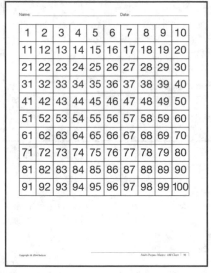

Extra Support: Number Lines, Masters Booklet p. 34

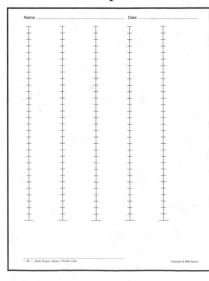

2 Grouping to Divide

 Goal Divide by counting equal groups.

Prerequisite Skills/Concepts

- Skip count by 2s to 7s.
- Use a number line.
- Divide by sharing.

Expectations

3m4 understand and explain basic operations ([addition, subtraction, multiplication,] division) involving whole numbers by modelling and discussing a variety of problem situations

3m6 develop proficiency in [multiplying and] dividing one-digit whole numbers

3m23 interpret [multiplication and] division sentences in a variety of ways

3m27 demonstrate and recall [multiplication facts to 7 × 7 and] division facts to 49 ÷ 7 using concrete materials

3m88 identify relationships between [addition, subtraction,] multiplication, and division

Assessment for Feedback	What You Will See Students Doing...	
Students will	**When Students Understand**	**If Students Misunderstand**
• skip count backward by a variety of numbers	• Students will skip count backward accurately by each number (e.g., skip count backward by 2s: 10, 8, 6, 4, 2, 0).	• Students who lose their place when skip counting or who rely on counting backward by 1s would benefit from using a number line.
• write division sentences	• Students will write division sentences using the correct numbers in the right sequence (e.g., 10 ÷ 5 = 2).	• Students may use the correct numbers in the division sentence, but not write the numbers in the correct sequence (e.g., 5 ÷ 10 = 2). Connect the number sentence to the language: "10 counters divided into groups of 5 is 2 groups."
• explain how subtraction and division are related	• Students will show that using groups for the same number of objects is the same as subtracting the same number from a total number of objects (e.g., in the case of 10 ÷ 2 = 5, they might proceed as follows: 10 − 2 − 2 − 2 − 2 − 2 = 0. You needed to subtract 2 five times to get to 0. You need 5 groups of 2 to make 10).	• Students may misinterpret a repeated subtraction sentence. Assist them in writing a repeated subtraction while dividing counters into groups. Then relate the groups and the subtraction sentence to the division sentence.

Preparation and Planning

Pacing	**5–10 min** Introduction **10–15 min** Teaching and Learning **10–15 min** Consolidation
Materials	• counters • (optional) calculators
Masters	• (for Extra Support) 100 Chart, Masters Booklet p. 31 • (for Extra Support) Number Lines, Masters Booklet p. 34 • (for Extra Support of Questions 5–8) Scaffolding p. 59
Workbook	p. 78
Vocabulary/ Symbols	skip counting, division, grouping
Key Assessment of Learning Question	Question 6, Understanding of Concepts

Meeting Individual Needs

Extra Challenge

- Students might list numbers divisible by 2 and by 5. They may then figure out what numbers are divisible by both 2 and 5, and try to find a pattern created by these numbers.

Extra Support

- Some students may continue to need 100 charts and number lines to assist with skip counting.
- Provide calculators to assist students in skip counting backward.

1. Introduction (Whole Class)
▶ 5–10 min

Ask four to eight students to remove their shoes and place them in one large pile.

- One student counts the total number of shoes.
- Another student guesses and then divides shoes into pairs (groups of 2).
- Another student estimates and then counts the number of pairs of shoes.

Write a division sentence for the situation on the board.

Hand out 15 to 20 counters to students. Ask them to model the shoe answer.

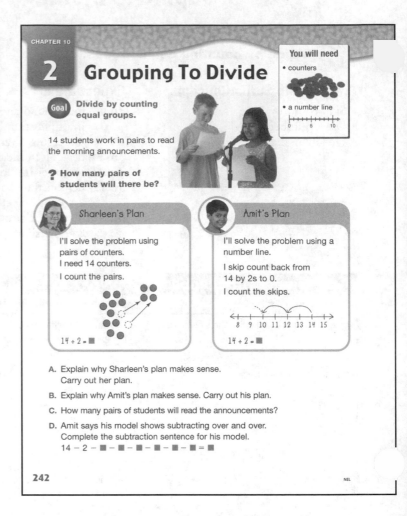

2. Teaching and Learning (Whole Class) ▶ 15 min

Together, read the opening statement and central question on Student Book page 242. Ask students how this is similar to the shoe problem from the Introduction. Read Sharleen's and Amit's plans and discuss how each plan helps to answer the central question. Compare the similarities and differences between Sharleen's plan and Amit's plan. Have students use counters to respond to prompts A, B, and C.

Read and discuss prompt D. As students begin to respond, model their replies on the board so that they can visually connect subtraction with division.

Reflecting

Have students connect Questions 1 and 2 on Student Book page 243 with the two plans on Student Book page 242. When answering Question 3, ensure that a visual model is available for students so they can see that one student will be left over.

Sample Discourse

1. • *You can skip count by 2s, from 0 up to 14, so Sharleen's model could show multiplication, too.*

- *Sharleen's model shows 14 ÷ 2 = 7, but it also shows 7 × 2 = 14. You could use the same counters grouped the same way to show either division or multiplication.*
- *When Sharleen counts pairs, it is like skip counting by 2s: 0, 2, 4, 6, 8, 10, 12, 14. So 7 × 2 = 14.*

2. • *My repeated subtraction sentence is like taking counters away two at a time. I'll have 2 counters in each group and I'll have 7 groups, so that's like 14 ÷ 2 = 7.*

- *If you start with 14 and subtract 2s, you can subtract 7 times: 14, 12, 10, 8, 6, 4, 2, 0. So 14 ÷ 2 = 7. Subtracting over and over is like division.*

3. • *Everything's the same except that now you have one student left over.*

- *You still divide the same way. You can use counters like Sharleen or skip counting like Amit. If you skip count, you would go 15, 13, 11, 9, 7, 5, 3, 1. You're not at 0, but you can't skip count anymore. So you just have to put up with that one.*
- *There will be 7 pairs. This is different from finding pairs for 14 because that comes out evenly.*

Reflecting

1. How does Sharleen's model show multiplication as well as division?

2. How is your repeated subtraction sentence like the division sentence?

3. If 15 students read the announcements, how many pairs would there be?
   How is this different from finding pairs for 14?

Checking

4. 24 students run in relay teams of 4.
   a) How many teams are there? Model your solution with counters and with skip counting on a number line.
   b) Write a division sentence to represent the students in teams. What is the quotient?

Practising

5. How many groups of 7 line dancers could you make? Model the groups with counters or number lines. Write a division sentence.
   a) 21 dancers
   b) 35 dancers

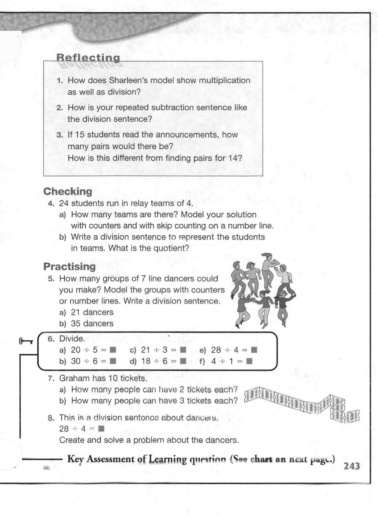

6. Divide.
   a) $20 \div 5 = \blacksquare$ c) $21 \div 3 = \blacksquare$ e) $28 \div 4 = \blacksquare$
   b) $30 \div 6 = \blacksquare$ d) $18 \div 6 = \blacksquare$ f) $4 \div 1 = \blacksquare$

7. Graham has 10 tickets.
   a) How many people can have 2 tickets each?
   b) How many people can have 3 tickets each?

8. This is a division sentence about dancers.
   $28 \div 4 = \blacksquare$
   Create and solve a problem about the dancers.

——— Key Assessment of Learning question (See chart on next page.)

243

---

3. Consolidation ▶ 10–15 min

For intervention strategies, refer to Meeting Individual Needs and the Assessment for Feedback chart.

Checking (Small Groups/Pairs)

4. You might ask students to model this using counters or students themselves, if you have enough. Have students compare their answers with those found by another group or the whole class.

Practising (Individual)

5–8. Encourage students to use both counters and number line skip counting as their strategies for calculating the answers. If students require Extra Support, provide copies of **Scaffolding Master p. 59**.

Closing (Whole Class)

Discuss the similarity between grouping and sharing (discussed in the previous lesson) as methods of division. Review briefly what happens when division is not even.

Answers

A. For example, Sharleen will use 14 counters and put them in groups of 2. Then she can count the groups. 14 counters in groups of 2 gives 7 groups: $14 \div 2 = 7$.

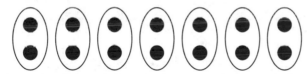

B. For example, Amit will start at 14 on the number line and keep skipping by 2s until he gets back to 0. Then he can count the skips. Starting at 14 and skipping back by 2s gives 7 jumps: $14 \div 2 = 7$.

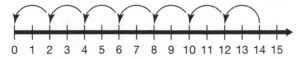

C. 7

D. $14 - 2 - 2 - 2 - 2 - 2 - 2 - 2 = 0$

1.–3. See sample answers under Reflecting.

4. a) 6; for example:

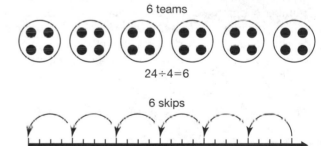

6 teams

$24 \div 4 = 6$

6 skips

$24 \div 4 = 6$

b) $24 \div 4 = 6$. The quotient is 6.

(Lesson 2 Answers continued on p. 67)

Assessment Strategy: short answer
Understanding of Concepts

Question 6
- Divide.

    a) 20 ÷ 5 = ■   **b)** 30 ÷ 6 = ■   **c)** 21 ÷ 3 = ■   **d)** 18 ÷ 6 = ■   **e)** 28 ÷ 4 = ■   **f)** 4 ÷ 1 = ■
    (Score correct responses out of 6.)

Extra Practice and Extension

- You might assign any of the questions related to this lesson, which are cross-referenced in the chart below.

Mid-Chapter Review	Student Book p. 246, Question 2
Skills Bank	Student Book pp. 254–255, Questions 5–7
Chapter Review	Student Book p. 257, Questions 2 & 3
Workbook	p. 78, all questions
Nelson Web Site	Visit **www.mathk8nelson.com** and follow the links to *Nelson Mathematics 3*, Chapter 10.

Math Background

Dividing through grouping is slightly different than sharing. Grouping means splitting a large group of objects into groups of a specific number. An example of grouping is calculating how many groups are needed if there are a total of 20 students and 5 people are in each group. You already know the number to be placed in each group. Division through grouping is likened to taking groups of a specific size away from the total. Mathematically, it is like skip counting backward by various numbers (2s, 3s, 4s, 5s...) to separate the total number into equal groups. A total number of objects divided into groups of a specific size tells you the number of groups. It is not critical that students be able to tell you exactly what kind of dividing they are doing, but rather that they recognize both types of problems as division problems.

Common Misconceptions: Students also may continue to confuse the divisor and the dividend when recording their questions.

At Home

- Students might check around the house to find objects that come in different numbered sets (e.g., two eggs in a tray, three bags of milk, four rolls of hockey tape, and so on). They can create simple division problems involving grouping of these objects. For example, golf balls can be purchased in boxes of 12. If each person gets two, how many people will receive golf balls?

Extra Support:
Scaffolding Master p. 59

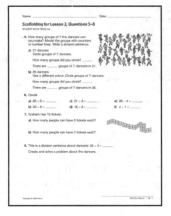

Extra Support:
100 Chart,
Masters Booklet p. 31

Extra Support:
Number Lines,
Masters Booklet p. 34

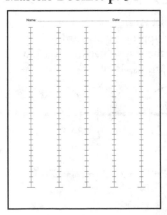

3 Communicate About Division

Goal Use a model to explain how to divide.

Prerequisite Skills/Concepts

- Use counters and number lines to skip count backward by 2s, 5s, and 10s.
- Divide by sharing and grouping.
- Explore division problems (sharing) using concrete materials.

Expectations

3m4 understand and explain basic operations ([addition, subtraction, multiplication,] division) involving whole numbers by modelling and discussing a variety of problem situations

3m8 solve problems and describe and explain the variety of strategies used

3m23 interpret multiplication and division sentences in a variety of ways

Assessment for Feedback	What You Will See Students Doing...	
Students will	**When Students Understand**	**If Students Misunderstand**
• explain how to divide	• Students will model division with concrete materials and explain the process orally and through pictures, numbers, and words, the process of dividing one number by another.	• Students may model division with the correct number of objects, but not in the correct groupings. Provide plates or circles on paper for them to organize the groups.

Preparation and Planning

Pacing	**5–10 min** Introduction **15–20 min** Teaching and Learning **20–30 min** Consolidation
Materials	• counters
Masters	• (for Extra Support) 100 Chart, Masters Booklet p. 31 • (for Extra Support) Number Lines, Masters Booklet p. 34
Workbook	p. 79
Key Assessment of Learning Question	Question 4, Communication

Meeting Individual Needs

Extra Challenge

- Students might create their own questions involving communicating about division. They may want to exchange and solve another student's problem, using the Communication Checklist as their guide.

Extra Support

- Some students may require the use of a calculator, a number line, counters, or a 100 chart to divide or skip count backward.
- Students who have difficulty writing their answers will benefit from an opportunity to provide oral responses.

Introduction (Whole Class)
♦ 5–10 min

Show students 15 apples (or other available objects) and three bowls or baskets. Explain that you would like to put the same number of apples in each container and ask for suggestions about how this can be done. Try out suggestions until you have five apples in each basket, and then ask:

- Are the groups equal? How do you know?
- When you take a number of things and put them in equal groups, are you adding, subtracting, multiplying, or dividing?
- What division sentence tells what we did?

$15 \div 3 = 5$ and $15 \div 5 = 3$ both describe the situation, but they tell different things about the apples. In $15 \div 3 = 5$, the quotient tells how many apples are in each basket. In $15 \div 5 = 3$, the quotient tells how many baskets there are. Ask students which piece of information they already knew, and which one they needed to find out.

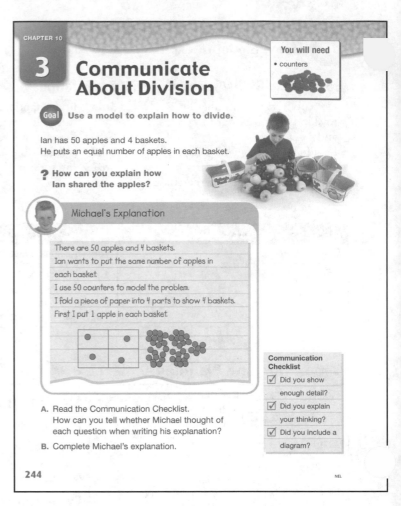

Teaching and Learning (Whole Class) ♦ 15–20 min

Direct students to look at the problem on Student Book page 244. Ian wants to share 50 apples in 4 baskets. Read Michael's Explanation about sharing these apples. Have students use the Communication Checklist to respond to prompt A and discuss Michael's strategy for solving this problem. Have students respond to prompt B individually or in pairs, and then compare answers as a whole class.

Reflecting

Questions 1 and 2 give students an opportunity to see the importance of establishing a connection between pictures and words. Students should have a chance to assess the strengths and the places where improvement in the answer could be demonstrated.

Sample Discourse

1. • *Michael's picture shows the four groups and the apples. It's easier than words or numbers and it helps you get started thinking about the problem yourself.*

• *You could imagine apples and baskets but it gets pretty hard to think about. You could draw apples and baskets but that's a lot of drawing. Michael's idea was smart—he used counters for apples and paper for baskets. That's easier to work with; and when it came time for him to do his picture, it was easier to draw, too.*

2. • *I thought my explanation was good because I just kept on doing what Michael was doing—only I went further. I showed all the apples sorted into baskets, except the last two.*

• *I had a lot of detail at first, but when I finished my diagram, I was able to go back and cut some detail out. My diagram was good because it showed how many counters were in each box—I guess you'd say how many apples in each basket. My diagram showed there were two left over, but I explained that. I'm not a good artist, so my diagram wasn't that good, but it was neat and you could see what was happening.*

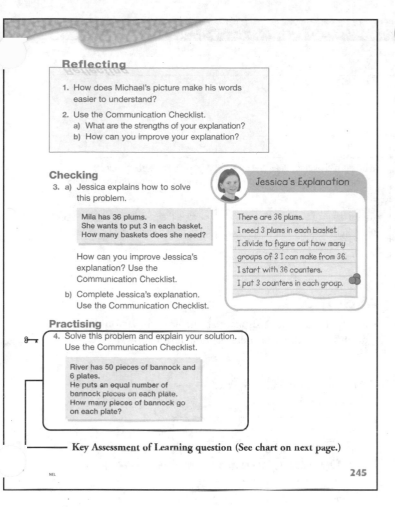

Reflecting

1. How does Michael's picture make his words easier to understand?

2. Use the Communication Checklist.
   a) What are the strengths of your explanation?
   b) How can you improve your explanation?

Checking

3. a) Jessica explains how to solve this problem.

   Jessica's Explanation

   > Mila has 36 plums.
   > She wants to put 3 in each basket.
   > How many baskets does she need?

   > There are 36 plums.
   > I need 3 plums in each basket.
   > I divide to figure out how many groups of 3 I can make from 36.
   > I start with 36 counters.
   > I put 3 counters in each group.

   How can you improve Jessica's explanation? Use the Communication Checklist.

   b) Complete Jessica's explanation. Use the Communication Checklist.

Practising

4. Solve this problem and explain your solution. Use the Communication Checklist.

   > River has 50 pieces of bannock and 6 plates.
   > He puts an equal number of bannock pieces on each plate.
   > How many pieces of bannock go on each plate?

   ── **Key Assessment of Learning question (See chart on next page.)**

---

3. Consolidation ⬧ 20–30 min

Checking (Pairs or Small Groups)

For intervention strategies, refer to Meeting Individual Needs and the Assessment for Feedback chart.

3. Discuss the strengths of Jessica's explanation and the places where she could improve. Compare her explanation to Michael's explanation on Student Book page 244.

Practising (Individual)

4. You may want to read this question together. Remind students to use pictures, words, and numbers in their solutions. Students should make use of concrete materials, such as counters, number lines, 100 charts, multiplication tables, or calculators, to do their calculations.

   Note that any answer from 1 to 8 pieces of bannock on each plate is acceptable, since the question does not specify that there cannot be lots left over.

   Watch students as they work with Question 4 to see if anyone puts the counters into piles of six. If so, talk about how you still get the right answer if you do this, but the model doesn't look quite right because you end up with eight plates, not six. Talk about the difference between sharing and grouping (as discussed in the previous two lessons).

Answers

A. For example:

☑ Did you show enough detail?	I think Michael showed a lot of detail because he used words and numbers and pictures. He told about what Ian already knew and what he needed to find out, and he showed the steps Ian used to figure out the answer.
☑ Did you explain your thinking?	Michael explained how Ian knew to use division, why he used 50 counters, and why he folded the paper into four parts.
☑ Did you include a diagram?	Michael used a diagram to show how Ian shared the first 4 apples in the 4 paper baskets.

B. For example, then I put one more apple in each basket. I kept doing this until there were no more groups of 4 left. I found out that I can put 12 apples in each basket, but 2 are left over.

1. For example, modelling the apples with counters and the baskets with paper makes the problem really simple; we don't have to worry about apples and baskets, just the division. The diagram shows how to actually use his model.

2. a) For example, I like the way I used a diagram to show 12 counters in each section. I also remembered to put a sentence at the end to tell my answer to the problem.

   b) For example, I could write the number sentence $50 \div 4 = 12$ with my counter picture to show what it means.

3. a) For example:

☑ Did you show enough detail?	Jessica remembered to explain what the problem told her and what she had to find out. She told how many counters she used and showed how she started to group them.
☑ Did you explain your thinking?	Jessica explained why she divided and why she started with 36 counters.
☑ Did you include a diagram?	Jessica used a diagram to show how she made the first group of three counters.

   b) For example, then I made more groups of 3. I kept going until no counters were left. I found out that I can make 12 groups of 3. $36 \div 3 = 12$. Jessica needs 12 baskets because she can make 12 groups of 3.

4. For example, there are 50 pieces of bannock. There are 6 plates. I divide to find out how many pieces of bannock I can put on each plate. I draw 6 plates on a sheet of paper. Then I get 50 counters because there are 50 pieces of bannock. I put one counter on each plate. I keep on doing this until I can't add a counter to all 6 plates. I have put 8 counters on each plate, and 2 counters are left over. $50 \div 6 = 8$ with 2 left over.

Assessment Strategy: written question
Communication

Question 4

• Solve this problem and explain your solution. Use the Communication Checklist.
  River has 50 pieces of bannock and 6 plates. He puts an equal number of bannock pieces on each plate.
  How many pieces of bannock go on each plate?

1	2	3	4
• provides an incomplete or inaccurate explanation of thinking that lacks clarity or logical thought	• provides a partial explanation of thinking that shows some clarity and logical thought	• provides a complete, clear, and logical explanation of thinking	• provides a thorough, clear, and insightful explanation of thinking
• uses a diagram that exhibits minimal clarity and accuracy, and is ineffective in communicating	• uses a diagram that lacks clarity and accuracy, though not sufficient to impede communication	• uses a diagram that is sufficiently clear and accurate to communicate	• uses a diagram that is clear, precise, and effective in communicating

Extra Practice and Extension

• You might assign any of the questions related to this lesson, which are cross-referenced in the chart below.

Mid-Chapter Review	Student Book p. 246, Question 6
Workbook	p. 79, all questions
Nelson Web Site	Visit **www.mathk8.nelson.com** and follow the links to *Nelson Mathematics 3*, Chapter 10.

Math Background

When students are communicating about division, it is important that they use the language of sharing things into a specific number of groups or making groups of specific sizes. When they read division sentences, though, the language is the same. For example, $24 \div 6 = 4$ is always read as "24 divided by 6 is 4." This can represent 24 divided into 6 groups, and each group comes out to have a size of 4. Or it can mean 24 divided into groups of size 6, which means there can be 4 groups. Some students might hear others use the language "6 goes into 24 four times." Notice that the order of numbers does not match the sentence $24 \div 6 = 4$, and this may cause confusion.

At Home

• Students can communicate about how they would share 20 apples with the members of their family.

Extra Support: 100 Chart, Masters Booklet p. 31

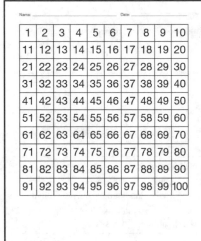

Extra Support: Number Lines, Masters Booklet p. 34

Mid-Chapter Review

Using the Mid-Chapter Review

Use this page to assess students' understanding of the concepts developed in the chapter so far. Refer to the assessment chart on pages 26–27 for the details of each question.

Materials: counters, number lines

1. & 3. Remind students to read carefully. Some problems require pictures, words, and numbers.

3. As an assessment of Lesson 2, the models should be the selection of equal groups, not sharing. However, you may want to indicate a different mix of models—some sharing and some selecting equal groups. Alternatively, by providing no prompts for students, you will be able to determine which meanings are preferred by different students—possibly useful assessment information.

6. Remind students of the Communication Checklist by posting a large checklist on the board, providing students with their own checklists, and reviewing questions orally with the class.

- ☐ Did you show enough detail?
- ☐ Did you explain your thinking?
- ☐ Did you include a diagram?

Related Questions to Ask

Ask	Possible Response
About **Question 3:** • What two meanings of division can your pictures show? (See the suggestion above for Question 3.)	• The pictures can show sharing equally into groups and selecting or removing of equal groups.
About **Question 4:** • What meanings of division does your picture show? (See the suggestion above for Question 3.)	• It can show sharing equally into groups or selecting of equal groups. (It may be necessary for students to describe the process used.)
About **Question 5:** • How can you use multiplication to solve this problem?	• Select any quotient—say 3. Multiply it by itself, $3 \times 3 = 9$. Rewrite as the division sentence $9 \div 3 = 3$.
About **Question 6:** • What questions can help you provide the details needed to answer this question?	• Did you show enough detail? Did you explain your thinking? Did you include a diagram?

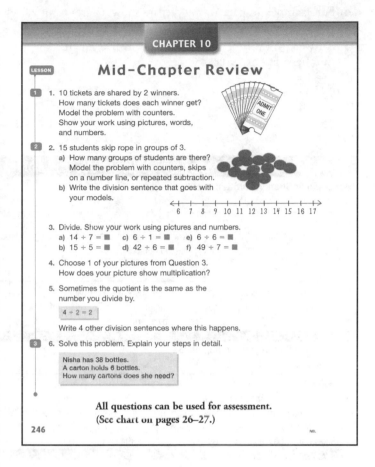

Answers

1. Each winner gets 5 tickets.

☐☐☐☐☐ ☐☐☐☐☐
$$10 \div 2 = 5$$

2. a) 5 groups   **b)** $15 \div 3 = 5$

3. a) 2

b) 3

c) 6

d) 7

e) 1

f) 7

4. For example, in part a), my picture shows 7 groups of 2; $7 \times 2 = 14$.

5. Answers will vary. The solutions all involve square numbers. For example:
$$1 \div 1 = 1$$
$$9 \div 3 = 3$$
$$16 \div 4 = 4$$
$$25 \div 5 = 5$$

6. For example, there are 38 bottles. 6 bottles go in each carton. I start with 38 bottles and make groups of 6. I make 6 groups with 2 left over. That's 6 cartons. Nisha will need another carton to carry the 2 leftover bottles. So she needs 7 cartons altogether.

Assessment of Learning—What to Look for in Student Work...

Assessment Strategy: written question
Understanding of Concepts

Question 1
- 10 tickets are shared by 2 winners. How many tickets does each winner get? Model the problem with counters. Show your work using pictures, words, and numbers.

1	2	3	4
• demonstrates an inaccurate understanding of division by sharing	• demonstrates a growing but still incomplete understanding of division by sharing	• demonstrates grade-appropriate understanding of division by sharing	• demonstrates in-depth understanding of division by sharing

Assessment Strategy: written question
Understanding of Concepts

Question 2
- 15 students skip rope in groups of 3.
  a) How many groups of students are there? Model the problem with counters, skips on a number line, or repeated subtraction.
  b) Write the division sentence that goes with your models.
  (Score 1 point for a correct model and 1 point for the correct division sentence, for a total of 2.)

Assessment Strategy: written question
Understanding of Concepts

Question 3
- Divide. Show your work using pictures and numbers.
  a) $14 \div 7 = \blacksquare$ **c)** $6 \div 1 = \blacksquare$ **e)** $6 \div 6 = \blacksquare$
  b) $15 \div 5 = \blacksquare$ **d)** $42 \div 6 = \blacksquare$ **f)** $49 \div 7 = \blacksquare$
  (Score 1 point for each correct picture model and 1 point for each correct number model, for a total of 12.)

Assessment Strategy: written question
Communication

Question 4
- Choose one of your pictures from Question 3. How does your picture show multiplication?

1	2	3	4
• provides an incomplete explanation that lacks clarity or logical thought	• provides a partial explanation that exhibits some clarity and logical thought	• provides a complete, clear, and logical explanation for how the picture shows multiplication	• provides a thorough, clear, and insightful explanation for how the picture shows multiplication

Assessment Strategy: short answer
Application of Procedures

Question 5
- Sometimes the quotient is the same as the number you divide by: $4 \div 2 = 2$
  Write 4 other division sentences where this happens.
  (Score correct responses out of 4.)

Assessment Strategy: short answer
Communication

Question 6
- Solve this problem. Explain your steps in detail.
  Nisha has 38 bottles. A carton holds 6 bottles. How many cartons does she need?

1	2	3	4
• provides an incomplete or inaccurate explanation of thinking that lacks clarity or logical thought	• provides a partial explanation of thinking that shows some clarity and logical thought	• provides complete, clear, and logical explanation of thinking	• provides a thorough, clear, and insightful explanation of thinking

Math Game: Fill-a-Row-Division

Using the Math Game

Materials: about 50 counters per game, 1 number line per game, minimum of 3 sets of number cards (preferably laminated or mounted) per game, for beginning play: 1 set of Beginning Division Strips (preferably laminated or mounted) per game, for regular play: 1 set of Mixed Division Strips with the numbers out of order (see Masters)

Masters: Beginning Division Strips p. 62, Mixed Division Strips p. 63, Number Cards p. 64

Object of the Game

Students will practise division facts, each player focusing on a specific divisor. To win at Fill-a-Row Division, one player must have covered an entire strip with a set of number cards (1 to 7). To make certain that appropriate strategies are being used, observe and discuss as noted below and refer students to the appropriate variation.

When to Play

Students can begin to play this game once they have completed Lessons 1 to 3 and the Mid-Chapter Review. Play may continue throughout the unit or school year.

Strategies

The strategies used will vary with the knowledge of the players. At first, students will likely use counters or the number line, and should be encouraged to play cooperatively —assisting each other with the materials and with placement of the cards.

A guessing-and-testing approach would involve making a series of totals with counters and sharing these into piles based on the divisor on the number strip.

A combined multiplication and materials approach could involve using the divisor as the number of groups and the number card drawn as the number in each group (or vice versa).

The most sophisticated strategy is to multiply the stated divisor by the number on the card.

Warning—an inappropriate but effective and simple strategy is for students to place a number card by counting along the strip by the number indicated. If this is observed, move students to variation 2.

Observe

Watch for students who do the following:
- place number cards by counting along the strip (see variation 2)
- use a guessing-and-testing approach, but have difficulty with larger numbers (see variation 3)
- continue to use materials for division facts they already know (point out that this is not necessary)

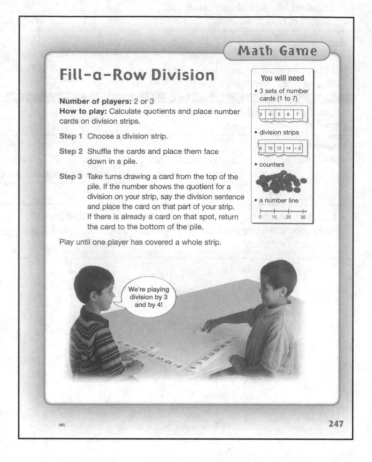

Discuss

After the game, ask students the following:
- How do you each decide how to place your number cards?
- Do you use counters, number lines, or mental math?
- Do you use multiplication, guess and test, or some other strategy?
- Did playing the game help you remember any of your division or multiplication facts?

Variations

- **Variation 1:** More than two or three students can play at one time. Either form teams or provide more sets of number cards and division strips.

- **Variation 2:** At some point, students may realize that number cards can be placed by merely counting along the division strip. Use the Mixed Division Strips when students have come to this realization.

- **Variation 3:** For an easier game, block out the larger numbers on the division strips and adjust the number cards used to fit the altered strips.

4 Exploring Division Patterns

 Goal Identify, describe, and extend division patterns.

Prerequisite Skills/Concepts

- Skip count forward and backward by 2s, 3s, 4s, 5s, 6s, 7s, and 10s.
- Identify number patterns used in counting.

Expectations

3m6 develop proficiency in multiplying and dividing one-digit whole numbers

3m14 count backwards by 2s, 5s, and 10s [from 100 using multiples of 2, 5, and 10 as starting points and by 100s from any number less than 1001]

3m24 identify numbers that are divisible by 2, 5, or 10

3m27 demonstrate and recall [multiplication facts to 7×7 and] division facts to $49 \div 7$ using concrete materials

3m32 use appropriate strategies to solve number problems involving whole numbers

3m88 identify relationships between [addition, subtraction,] multiplication, and division

Assessment for Feedback	What You Will See Students Doing...	
Students will	**When Students Understand**	**If Students Misunderstand**
• skip count backward by a variety of numbers	• Students will show skip counting accurately by 2s, 5s, and 10s on a 100 chart.	• Students may count backward by 1s on the 100 chart to find the skip-counting patterns, and may make errors in counting. Encourage them to skip count forward by 2s, 5s, and 10s, and reinforce the patterns orally.
• identify counting patterns involving division (repeated subtraction)	• Students will use a number chart to identify counting patterns.	• Although students may locate the numbers on a 100 chart, they will not be able to identify the pattern they see. Encourage students to look for similarities and repetitions of the last digit of the number.

Preparation and Planning

Pacing	5–10 min Introduction 15–20 min Teaching and Learning 20–30 min Consolidation
Materials	• pencil crayons • large number line for the floor
Masters	• (for Extra Support) 100 Chart, Masters Booklet p. 31 • (for Extra Support) Number Lines, Masters Booklet p. 34
Workbook	• p.80
Key Assessment of Learning Question	Entire exploration, Problem Solving

Meeting Individual Needs

Extra Challenge

- Challenge students to find other division patterns on a 100 chart, using a different colour to identify each. Ask students if there are any similarities between patterns. Students can record and describe their patterns on chart paper for others to see, entitling them with catchy names such as Thrifty Threes, Fascinating Fours, Slick Sixes, and so on.

Extra Support

- Even though a visual chart has been used, some students need to connect physically with the pattern. Walking it out on a large number line on the floor may help.

1. Introduction (Whole Class)
▶ 5–10 min

Ask students to recall some of the patterns they have discovered when studying multiplication facts. Challenge them to suggest possible patterns for division facts.

Sample Discourse

"If we know that multiplication patterns are repeated addition of the same number, then what might division patterns be like?"

- *Addition is kind of the opposite of subtraction, so maybe division is the opposite of multiplication.*
- *Division patterns are like subtracting the same number over and over.*

"$4 \times 2 = 8$ means $2 + 2 + 2 + 2 = 8$. What does $8 \div 2 = 4$ mean?"

- *You can take four groups of 2 from 8.*
- *You can start at 8 and skip count backward by 2s. You can do it 4 times before you get to 0.*
  $8 - 2 - 2 - 2 - 2 = 0$

2. Teaching and Learning
(Whole Class/Individual) ▶ 15–20 min

Encourage a discussion of number patterns, using the 100 chart. Have students explain about the patterns they have discovered in division. As a class, read Student Book page 248, discussing the requirements of each question. Distribute a 100 chart to each student.

Ask students to choose distinct colours—some numbers will be coloured two or even three times. They should not fill in each square entirely with colour. Rather, they should make a single stroke (or example, a downward diagonal for Nicola's pattern, an upward diagonal for Robin's pattern, and a horizontal stroke for Mo's pattern). (See answers on the next page.) Alternatively, you might prefer to hand out three 100 charts—one for each pattern.

Some or all students may work in pairs as they read and discuss the questions. However, each student should complete a 100 chart.

Reflecting

In Questions 1 and 2, students apply what they have learned in prompts A to F to new numbers.

CHAPTER 10

4 Exploring Division Patterns

You will need
- a 100 chart

1	2	3	4
11	12	13	14
21	22	23	24

- pencil crayons

Goal Identify, describe, and extend division patterns.

? What pattern is used in each list?

A. Extend each pattern to 0. Write each pattern rule.

B. Colour each pattern on a 100 chart. Use 50 as the start number. Use a different colour for each pattern.

Nicola's pattern	Robin's pattern	Mo's pattern
50	50	50
40	45	48
30	40	46
20	35	44
■	■	■
■	■	■

C. Describe the patterns that you see on your 100 chart.

D. Nicola's pattern shows numbers that are all **divisible** by 10. What do you notice about the numbers?

E. Which pattern shows numbers that are all divisible by 2? What do you notice about the numbers?

F. Which pattern shows numbers that are all divisible by 5? What do you notice about the numbers?

> **divisible**
> Can be divided with nothing left over
> $40 \div 10 = 4$
> 40 is divisible by 10.

Reflecting

1. Which of these numbers are divisible by 10?
   30 35 77 80
   How do you know?

2. Which numbers that are divisible by 2 are also divisible by 5? Which are not?

248   **Entire exploration is for Assessment of Learning. (See chart on next page.)**   NEL

---

3. Consolidation (Whole Class)
▶ 20–30 min

For intervention strategies, refer to Meeting Individual Needs and the Assessment for Feedback chart.

Ask students "Why is it useful to identify and use patterns when dividing?" They can share their answers orally with the class or respond by writing in their journals.

Answers

A. For example:

	Pattern	Pattern rule
Nicola	50, 40, 30, 20, 10, 0	Start at 50 and subtract 10s until you get to 0.
Robin	50, 45, 40, 35, 30, 25, 20, 15, 10, 5, 0	Start at 50 and subtract 5s until you get to 0.
Mo	50, 48, 46, 44, 42, 40, 38, 36, 34, 32, 30, 28, 26, 24, 22, 20, 18, 16, 14, 12, 10, 8, 6, 4, 2, 0	Start at 50 and subtract 2s until you get to 0.

(Lesson 4 Answers continued on p. 68)

Assessment Strategy: investigation
The focus is on Problem Solving.

Assessment Opportunity
In this lesson, the entire exploration is an opportunity for assessment. You will see students carrying out an inquiry and will be able to observe their ability to use a 100 chart and pencil crayons to identify, describe, and extend division patterns. You will see them determine the divisibility of numbers.

To gather evidence about a student's ability to problem solve, use informal observation, questioning, and written work. Use the Problem-Solving Rubric (Tool 6) to help you focus on the problem-solving process. You may want to focus on the Carry Out the Plan, Look Back, and Communicate rows in the rubric.

Extra Practice and Extension

- You might assign any of the questions related to this lesson, which are cross-referenced in the chart below.

Mental Math	Student Book p. 249
Skills Bank	Student Book p. 255, Questions 9–11
Chapter Review	Student Book p. 257, Question 9
Workbook	p. 80, all questions
Nelson Web Site	Visit **www.mathk8nelson.com** and follow the links to *Nelson Mathematics 3*, Chapter 10.

Math Background

This is a lesson about patterns wherein students have opportunities to generalize similarities and/or differences about numbers coloured a certain way on a 100 chart. Students may first describe the physical patterns they see. Thereafter, they need to look at patterns in the digits. Remind them to talk about the location of certain digits using place-value language: for example, the ones place and the tens place.

At Home

- Students can search for numbers of things at home that are divisible by 2, 5, and 10. Opportunities depend to some extent upon the size of the family. If there are 5 people, there will be many things divisible by 5, like the number of chairs around the kitchen table or the number of utensils set on the table (15 utensils: 5 knives, 5 forks, 5 spoons). Someone's house number may be divisible by 2. Students may notice that all the houses on their side of the street or all the apartments their side of the hallway are divisible by 2.

**Extra Support: 100 Chart,
Masters Booklet p. 31**

**Extra Support: Number Lines,
Masters Booklet p. 34**

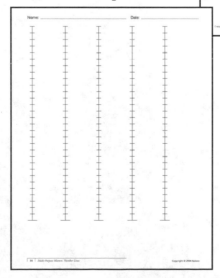

Mental Math: Using Equal Groups

Using Mental Math

Materials: number line

Place a number line on the board. Below the number line, write $3 + 3 + 3 + 3 = ?$

Ask students to use the number line to show how they arrive at the answer to this question. Now place the question $3 + 3 + 3 + 4 = ?$ on the board. Ask students how this question compares to the last one. Once again, refer to the number line to show the process for calculating the answer.

Refer to Student Book page 249. Read the information about Keisha's Multiplication. Have students explain her process. Compare it to Rachel's thinking in prompt A. Complete prompt B as a whole class or in pairs. Share answers as a whole class. Students may then complete Questions 1 and 2.

Answers

A. For example, Rachel saw the question as five 5s plus 1.

B. For example:
Keisha: I have 5 fours. $5 \times 4 = 20$ and add 3 more makes 23.
Rachel: I have $6 \times 4 = 24$ and subtract 1 makes 23.

1. a) $6 \times 4 = 24$, $24 + 3 = 27$ or $7 \times 4 = 28$, $28 - 1 = 27$

b) $7 \times 3 = 21$, $21 + 4 = 25$ or $8 \times 3 = 24$, $24 + 1 = 25$

2. a) 11

b) 36

c) 11

d) 28

e) 21

f) 14

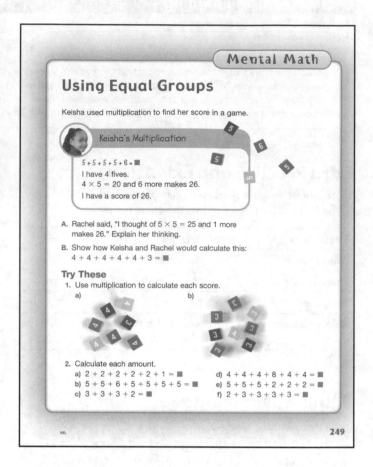

Mental Math

Using Equal Groups

Keisha used multiplication to find her score in a game.

Keisha's Multiplication

$5 + 5 + 5 + 5 + 6 = \blacksquare$
I have 4 fives.
$4 \times 5 = 20$ and 6 more makes 26.
I have a score of 26.

A. Rachel said, "I thought of $5 \times 5 = 25$ and 1 more makes 26." Explain her thinking.

B. Show how Keisha and Rachel would calculate this:
$4 + 4 + 4 + 4 + 4 + 3 = \blacksquare$

Try These

1. Use multiplication to calculate each score.
   a)   b)

2. Calculate each amount.
   a) $2 + 2 + 2 + 2 + 2 + 1 = \blacksquare$ d) $4 + 4 + 4 + 8 + 4 + 4 = \blacksquare$
   b) $5 + 5 + 6 + 5 + 5 + 5 + 5 = \blacksquare$ e) $5 + 5 + 5 + 2 + 2 + 2 = \blacksquare$
   c) $3 + 3 + 3 + 2 = \blacksquare$ f) $2 + 3 + 3 + 3 + 3 = \blacksquare$

NEL   249

5 Estimating Quotients

 Goal Solve division problems using estimation.

Prerequisite Skills/Concepts

- Skip count by 2s, 5s, and 10s.
- Solve problems using pictures, words, and numbers.
- Multiply to 7×7.

Expectations

3m6 develop proficiency in multiplying and dividing one-digit whole numbers

3m7 select and perform computation techniques ([addition, subtraction,] multiplication, division) appropriate to specific problems, and determine whether the results are reasonable

3m8 solve problems and describe and explain the variety of strategies used

3m27 demonstrate and recall [multiplication facts to 7×7 and] division facts to $49 \div 7$ using concrete materials

3m32 use appropriate strategies to solve number problems involving whole numbers

3m33 use various estimation strategies to solve problems, then check results for reasonableness

Assessment for Feedback	What You Will See Students Doing...	
Students will	**When Students Understand**	**If Students Misunderstand**
• solve problems involving division, using estimation	• Students will estimate answers to division problems using multiplication facts they know.	• Students may have difficulty recalling multiplication facts with products close to the given number. Encourage them to use counters, a number line, or a 100 chart.
• demonstrate division facts to $49 \div 7$	• Students accurately divide to $49 \div 7$, either mentally or using number lines, 100 charts, or counters.	• Students may have difficulty demonstrating division facts. Encourage them to show groups of counters and say a multiplication fact to match the groups. Relate the multiplication fact to the corresponding division fact.

Preparation and Planning

Pacing	**10–15 min** Introduction **10–20 min** Teaching and Learning **20–25 min** Consolidation
Materials	• play coins (loonies) • counters
Masters	• (for Extra Support) 100 Chart, Masters Booklet p. 31 • (for Extra Support) Number Lines, Masters Booklet p. 34 • (for Extra Support of Questions 5–7) Scaffolding p. 60
Workbook	p. 81
Key Assessment of Learning Question	Question 7, Understanding of Concepts

Meeting Individual Needs

Extra Challenge

- Students can create their own posters to display opportunities for estimating. These can relate to another area of the curriculum or a special event (for example, "Egg Decorating Kit—Good for 4 Dozen Eggs!"). They can display their posters, choose someone else's poster, and create an estimating problem. They can share problems and solutions with the class, using the posters as a backdrop for their presentations.

Extra Support

- Some students may need assistance in reading and completing the estimates.
- The use of a 100 chart or a calculator to answer each question will benefit some students.

Introduction (Whole Class)

▶ **10–15 min**

Present students with a pile of up to 15 counters. Ask students to estimate the number in the pile. Separate each pile into two roughly equal piles. Repeat the estimations. Present other estimating situations—starting with up to 22 counters, and then separating the counters into three or four roughly equal piles.

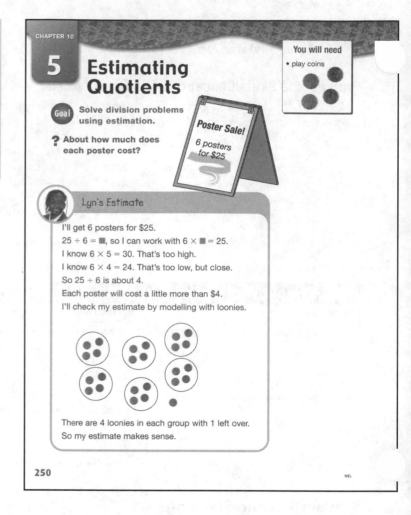

 Teaching and Learning (Small Group/Whole Class) ▶ **10–20 min**

Have students in small groups locate advertisements that show several items for one price (for example, 4 roast beef sandwiches for $19 or 3 pairs of shoes for $50).

Sample Discourse

Why do stores advertise several items for one price? "Is it cheaper to buy more?"
- *They want you to buy more and spend more.*
- *Each item might be cheaper than if you only bought them one at a time.*
- *Lots of times stores will give you a deal if you buy more.*

"How can you tell whether you are getting a deal?"
- *You can estimate. How many do you get for the sale price? Estimate the regular price for that many—if it is more, you're getting a deal.*

As a whole class, direct student attention to Student Book page 250. Read the poster and the central question together. Work through Lyn's estimate together, encouraging students to model the problem with play coins or counters.

Reflecting

Students are asked to think about Lyn's strategy. They also are given a chance to share other strategies that might be useful in calculating a reasonable estimate. Some students may want to make use of number lines, 100 charts, or calculators to do their estimates.

Sample Discourse

1. • *Lyn tries to think of a number to multiply because multiplying is easier than dividing.*
   • *She wants to multiply something by 6 because she's thinking of getting 6 posters.*

2. a) • *You would say "about 4" because it's not exactly 4, but it's close.*

   b) • *Another example might be that 35 divided by 6 is about 6 —because 6 × 6 is 36 and that's close.*
   • *44 divided by 6 is about 7—because 6 × 7 is 42. That's a little bit less, but not a lot less.*

Reflecting

1. Why does Lyn try to think of what number she can multiply by 6 to get close to 25?

2. a) Why would you say "about 4" to answer 25 ÷ 6?
   b) Give another example of when you might use an answer of "about" when dividing by 6.

Checking

3. Estimate. Use "about" in your answers. Explain your answers.
   a) 16 ÷ 3   b) 20 ÷ 3

4. a) 5 students are buying a gift for $22. About how much does each student have to pay? Show your work.
   b) With tax and gift wrap, the cost of the gift is $27. About how much does each student have to pay? Show your work.

Practising

5. Estimate. Write the number sentence you used for each estimate.
   a) 17 ÷ 5   c) 17 ÷ 6   e) 21 ÷ 6
   b) 34 ÷ 5   d) 35 ÷ 6   f) 30 ÷ 4

6. Estimate. Explain each estimate.
   a) the number of weeks in a month with 31 days
   b) 20 pencils shared by 7 children
   c) $52 to buy 7 posters

7. 3 teachers share 25 posters. About how many posters does each teacher get?

—— Key Assessment of Learning question (See chart on next page.) **251**

3. Consolidation ▶ 20–25 min

Checking (Pairs)

For intervention strategies, refer to Meeting Individual Needs box and Assessment for Feedback chart.

Option 1: Students work together to answer Questions 3 and 4. Remind them to discuss the strategy they used to arrive at an answer, and show their work to their partner so they can compare the similarities and the differences.

Option 2: Students work out the answers independently. Then they exchange, compare, and discuss their work in pairs.

Practising (Individual)

Remind students to show all of their work, especially in Questions 6 and 7. Some students should continue to make use of 100 charts or number lines.

5–7. For students who require Extra Support, provide copies of **Scaffolding Master p. 60**.

Closing (Whole Class)

Have students review strategies used to estimate of quotients. Ask the students how they used division and/or multiplication in their estimations.

Answers

1. Lyn multiplied by 6 because that is the number of posters that are on sale that she wants to buy.

2. a) For example, 25 ÷ 6 is about 4, not exactly 4. There are some left over.
   b) For example, when you divide 20 by 6, it is "about" 3.

3. a) For example, 16 ÷ 3 is about 5 because 15 ÷ 3 is exactly 5, and 16 is very close to 15.
   b) For example, 20 ÷ 3 is about 7 because 21 ÷ 3 is exactly 7, and 20 is very close to 21.

4. a) For example, 22 ÷ 5 = ■.
      4 × 5 = 20 (just a bit under 22) and 5 × 5 = 25 (just over 22)
      So 22 ÷ 5 = 4 and a bit more. Each student will pay a bit more than $4.
   b) For example, 5 × 5 = 25 so 27 ÷ 5 is a bit more than 5. Each student will pay a bit more than $5.

5. a) For example, about 3; number sentences: 3 × 5 = 15 or 15 ÷ 5 = 3
   b) For example, about 7; number sentences: 7 × 5 = 35 or 35 ÷ 5 = 7

   c) For example, about 3; 3 × 6 = 18 or 18 ÷ 6 = 3
   d) For example, about 7; 7 × 5 = 35 or 35 ÷ 5 = 7
   e) For example, about 3; 3 × 7 = 21 or 21 ÷ 7 = 3
   f) For example, about 7; 7 × 4 = 28 or 28 ÷ 4 = 7

6. a) For example, 31 ÷ 4 = ■.
      32 is close to 31 and 4 × 8 = 32.
      32 ÷ 4 = 8
      So 31 ÷ 4 is about 8 weeks.
   b) For example, 20 ÷ 7 = ■.
      21 is close to 20 and 7 × 3 = 21.
      21 ÷ 7 = 3
      So 20 ÷ 7 is about 3 pencils each.
   c) 52 ÷ 7 = ■.
      49 is close to 52 and 7 × 7 = 49.
      49 ÷ 7 = 7
      So 52 ÷ 7 is about $7 each.

7. For example, each teacher gets about 8 posters.

Assessment Strategy: written question
Understanding of Concepts

Question 7
• 3 teachers share 25 posters. About how many posters does each teacher get?

1	2	3	4
• has difficulty connecting new concept (e.g., division of whole numbers) to prior learning (e.g., using modelling to estimate)	• demonstrates a limited ability to connect new concept (e.g., division of whole numbers) to prior learning (e.g., using modelling to estimate)	• demonstrates a growing ability to connect new concept (e.g., division of whole numbers) to prior learning (e.g., using modelling to estimate)	• easily connects new concept (e.g., division of whole numbers) to prior learning (e.g., using modelling to estimate)

Extra Practice and Extension

• You might assign any of the questions related to this lesson, which are cross-referenced in the chart below.

Skills Bank	Student Book p. 255, Question 12
Problem Bank	Student Book p. 256, Questions 2, 5, & 7
Chapter Review	Student Book p. 257, Question 10
Workbook	p. 81, all questions
Nelson Web Site	**Visit www.mathk8nelson.com** and follow the links to *Nelson Mathematics 3*, Chapter 10.

Math Background

Estimating is a "reasoning-based" skill in math. Estimating requires number sense and process skills. Without training, students think that estimating is about guessing, and do not realize that people who make reasoned estimates use specific skills and processes.

In this lesson, it is important to emphasize the connection between multiplying and dividing. For example, when estimating 16 ÷ 3, remind students of the language of dividing by saying, "About how many times can 16 be grouped in 3s?"

Students may use multiplication tables, counters, or number lines when estimating division using multiplication facts.

At Home

• Students can look through newspapers or the weekly food flyers for advertisements to find examples where they can estimate the cost of one item, given the cost of several. (For example, 3 cases of pop cost $10. How much is 1 case? 2 pencils cost 23¢. How much is 1 pencil?)

**Extra Support: 100 Chart,
Masters Booklet p. 31**

**Extra Support:
Number Lines,
Masters Booklet p. 34**

**Extra Support:
Scaffolding Master p. 60**

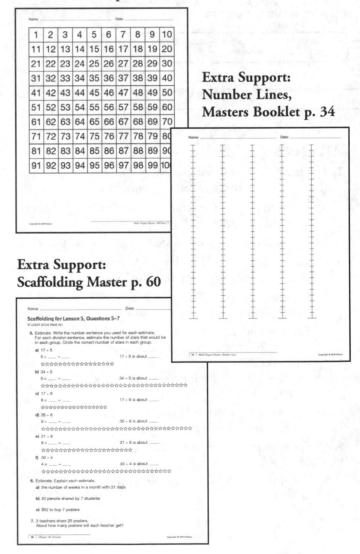

6 Division Strategies

 Goal Use estimation and multiplication to solve division problems with greater numbers.

Prerequisite Skills/Concepts

- Skip count backward by a variety of numbers.
- Multiply to 7×7.
- Estimate using multiplication and division.
- Use a calculator.

Expectations

3m6 develop proficiency in multiplying and dividing one-digit whole numbers

3m8 solve problems and describe and explain the variety of strategies used

3m10 use a calculator to solve problems beyond the required pencil-and-paper skills

3m22 use a calculator to examine number relationships and the effect of repeated operations on numbers

3m27 demonstrate and recall [multiplication facts to 7×7 and] division facts to $49 \div 7$ using concrete materials

3m32 use appropriate strategies to solve number problems involving whole numbers

3m88 identify relationships between [addition, subtraction,] multiplication, and division

Assessment for Feedback	What You Will See Students Doing...	
Students will	**When Students Understand**	**If Students Misunderstand**
• use estimation and multiplication to solve division problems	• Students will use multiplication to solve division problems.	• Students may require asistance to compare their estimates with the target number. Help them raise their estimates to get closer.
• use a calculator to work with larger numbers	• Students will use a calculator to answer problems with larger numbers. They will be able to press the correct function keys to complete the answer, correct their mistakes, and reset the calculator for a new problem.	• Some students may need assistance in operating the calculator. Remind them of specific calculator key functions, such as the clear key.

Preparation and Planning

Pacing	**5–10 min** Introduction **20–30 min** Teaching and Learning **15–20 min** Consolidation
Materials	• calculators
Masters	• (for Extra Support of Questions 5–9) Scaffolding p. 81
Workbook	p. 82
Vocabulary/ Symbols	estimation, metre (m), quotient, division, multiplication
Key Assessment of Learning Question	Question 6, Problem Solving

Meeting Individual Needs

Extra Challenge

- Students can research other tall buildings similar to the CN Tower, and estimate the number of equivalent two-storey heights. Try searching for "skyscraper" on the Internet.

Extra Support

- Students may have difficulty remembering the numbers they have entered into the calculator. Encourage them to record their entries. Some students may also benefit from working in pairs with a student who can model the division strategies or answer questions as they work through a question together.

1. Introduction (Small Group/ Whole Class) ▶ 5–10 min

Ask students what they know about the CN Tower. If necessary, provide information, such as the following:
- height: 553 m
- number of steps: 1776
- height of the observation deck: 342 m

Engage students in ballpark estimates related to this information by asking: "Is the height of the tower more or less than 1 km? About how many CN Towers would make a kilometre? About how many flights of stairs do you think are in 1776 steps?" Accept all estimates. Tell students that, in this lesson, they will learn a strategy for making closer estimates.

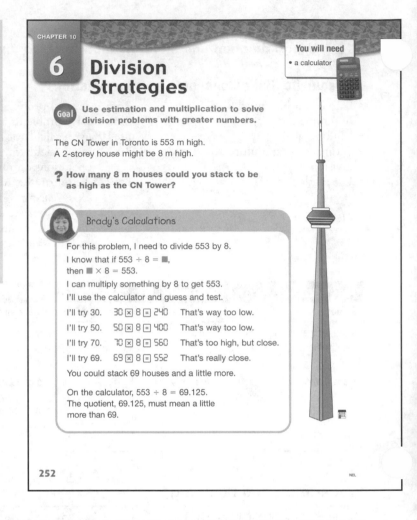

6 Division Strategies

You will need
- a calculator

Goal Use estimation and multiplication to solve division problems with greater numbers.

The CN Tower in Toronto is 553 m high.
A 2-storey house might be 8 m high.

? How many 8 m houses could you stack to be as high as the CN Tower?

Brady's Calculations

For this problem, I need to divide 553 by 8.
I know that if 553 ÷ 8 = ■,
then ■ × 8 = 553.
I can multiply something by 8 to get 553.
I'll use the calculator and guess and test.

I'll try 30. 30 × 8 = 240 That's way too low.
I'll try 50. 50 × 8 = 400 That's way too low.
I'll try 70. 70 × 8 = 560 That's too high, but close.
I'll try 69. 69 × 8 = 552 That's really close.

You could stack 69 houses and a little more.

On the calculator, 553 ÷ 8 = 69.125.
The quotient, 69.125, must mean a little more than 69.

252　　　　　　NEL

2. Teaching and Learning (Whole Class) ▶ 20–30 min

Draw attention to Student Book page 252. Read the introductory statement about the CN Tower and the related question below. Then read and discuss Brady's calculation. Have students follow the calculations using calculators of their own. Students who have difficulty following directions and keeping pace may benefit from working in pairs. Discuss the advantages of using a calculator to solve the problem. Students may take a long time to reach a close estimate. Encourage them to not give up and to write down their guesses so they don't repeat themselves.

Reflecting

In these questions, students have a chance to review the process Brady used to calculate the answer and the reason multiplication was used to solve a division question. Give students time to discuss these answers—first in small groups, and then as a whole class. Encourage a variety of answers.

Sample Discourse

1. • *Brady tried lots of numbers and finally got down to one guess that was really close.*
   • *She was guessing, but she had a strategy.*
   • *When her guess was low, she guessed a higher number, and when it was too high, she guessed a lower number.*
   • *She tested her guesses with a calculator.*

Reflecting

1. How do you think Brady decided what to guess each time?

2. Suppose Brady had tried 80 first. What would she have learned? What would she do next?

3. Why did Brady try different multiplications to solve a division question?

Checking

4. Mont Tremblant in Quebec is 968 m high. How many 8 m houses would stack up to be as high as Mount Tremblant?

Practising

5. 3 tennis balls can be stacked in a container. The tennis club collected 85 loose balls. How many containers would 85 balls fill?

6. 289 students need to divide themselves into 15 teams for play day. How many students will be on each team?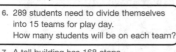

7. A tall building has 168 steps. There are 12 steps between floors. How many floors does the building have?

8. Jeff is 102 months old. How many years old is he?

9. Margaret's birthday is 100 days away. How many weeks away is her birthday?

— **Key Assessment of Learning question** (See chart on next page.) 253

---

3. Consolidation ▸ 15–20 min

Checking (Pairs)

For intervention strategies, refer to Meeting Individual Needs box and Assessment for Feedback chart.

Encourage students to work together in pairs, to use their calculators, and to record all of their guesses. This is a good opportunity to write the strategies/ guesses on the board and share the answers as a whole class.

Practising (Pairs/Individual)

Remind students to work in pairs if needed, and to record all of their guesses.

5–9. For students who require Extra Support, provide copies of **Scaffolding Master p. 61**.

Closing (Whole Class)

When students have completed Questions 5 to 9, have them look back at their answers and write in their journals, using prompts such as:

• "Using a calculator for these questions was helpful because…"

• "Writing down all of my guesses was important because…"

Answers

1. When Brady 's guess was low, she added to her guess. When she was too high she subtracted from her guess. If her multiplication was off by a lot, she changed her guess by a lot. If her multiplication was off by a little, she changed her guess by a little.

2. For example, if Brady had tried 80 first, she would have found that $80 \times 8 = 640$, which is too high. She would have tried a smaller number.

3. For example, division and multiplication are closely related. Brady used multiplication to find out that 69 groups of 8 make 552. Since 553 is only one more than 552, this told her that $553 \div 8$ is about 69.

4. 121 houses

5. 28 containers with 1 ball left over

6. For example, they could have 15 teams of 19 students with 4 left over, or they could have 4 teams of 20 and 11 teams of 19.

7. 14

8. 8

9. For example:
   7 days × 10 weeks = 70. That's too low.
   7 × 15 = 105. That's too high.
   7 × 14 = 98. That's the closest.
   Margaret's birthday is about 14 weeks away.

Assessment Strategy: written question
Problem Solving

Question 6
• 289 students need to divide themselves into 15 teams for play day. How many students will be on each team?

1	2	3	4
• uses a strategy and attempts to solve the problem, but does not arrive at an answer	• carries out the plan to some extent using a strategy, and develops a partial and/or incorrect solution	• carries out the plan effectively by using estimation and multiplication to solve a division problem with greater numbers	• shows flexibility and insight by using estimation and multiplication to solve a division problem with greater numbers

Extra Practice and Extension

• You might assign any of the questions related to this lesson, which are cross-referenced in the chart below.

Skills Bank	Student Book p. 255, Questions 13 & 14
Problem Bank	Student Book p. 256, Question 8
Workbook	p. 82, all questions
Nelson Web Site	Visit **www.mathk8nelson.com** and follow the links to *Nelson Mathematics 3*, Chapter 10.

Math Background

The purpose of this lesson is to engage students in dividing numbers greater than the $49 \div 7$ requirements for proficiency. Students begin to apply their dividing concepts to numbers that are outside the range of "facts." This is a good chance to reinforce the connections between division and multiplication. When students divide 553 by 8 on the calculator, they get an answer that they have not been taught to interpret. So they are shown how they might turn the question around and try to figure out what it could mean. By guessing and testing, they can use multiplication to answer the question.

Exploring and identifying remainders may give students insights into what the decimal part of that number they see on the calculator screen could mean. This will foreshadow the study of decimals and fractions.

At Home

• Students may look around the house and compare two to four very small objects with very tall objects. How many pennies does it take to make a chair leg? How many pencils does it take to reach the top of a wall? They can create a chart of their findings and share it with the class.

Extra Support:
Scaffolding Master p. 61

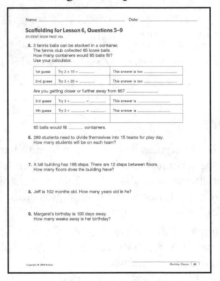

Skills Bank

Using the Skills Bank

Materials: counters, number lines

Remind students to read the instructions carefully. Several questions require more than a short answer.

1. & 3. These questions require pictures.

7. Let students know whether you require a picture for the model they have used.

9.–11. These questions require explanations as well as short answers.

12. Discuss how Lee provides his thinking for $23 \div 6$.

14. Let students know how extensive their explanations must be. Approaches to this question may vary. Some students will interpret the calculator answer using division. Others may use a guessing-and-testing approach, using the calculator for multiplication.

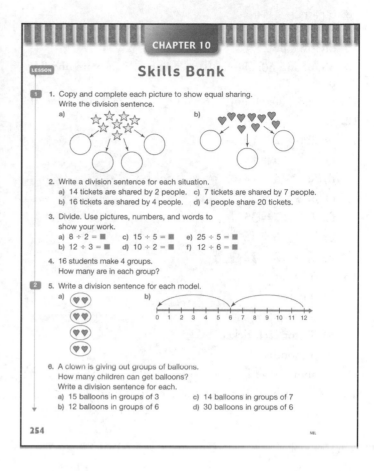

Answers

1. a) Each circle should have 2 stars. $8 \div 4 = 2$

   b) Each circle should have 3 hearts. $9 \div 3 = 3$

2. a) $14 \div 2 = 7$

   b) $16 \div 4 = 4$

   c) $7 \div 7 = 1$

   d) $20 \div 4 = 5$

3. a) 4

   b) 4

   c) 3

   d) 5

   e) 5

   f) 2

4. 4 students are in each group; $16 \div 4 = 4$.

5. a) $8 \div 2 = 4$

   b) $12 \div 6 = 2$

6. a) $15 \div 3 = 5$

   b) $12 \div 6 = 2$

   c) $14 \div 7 = 2$

   d) $30 \div 6 = 5$

7. a) 4

   b) 7

   c) 6

   d) 1

   e) 7

   f) 3

8. 6 pairs

9. 14 and 98; all even numbers (ending in 0, 2, 4, 6, 8) are divisible by 2

10. 45, 5, and 60; all numbers ending in 0 or 5 are divisible by 5

11. 90 and 100; all numbers ending in 0 are divisible by 10

12. a) 1; $6 \times 1 = 6$

   b) 2; $6 \times 2 = 12$

   c) 3; $6 \times 3 = 18$

   d) 5; $5 \times 5 = 25$

   e) 6; $6 \times 5 = 30$

   f) 7; $5 \times 7 = 35$

   g) 6; $7 \times 6 = 42$

   h) 6; $6 \times 2 = 12$

13. a) 6 hands

   b) 6 pairs

   c) 6 packs

   d) $7 for each ticket

   e) 3 months

   f) about 4 weeks

14. 9 cartons hold 108 eggs and 8 cartons hold 96 eggs.

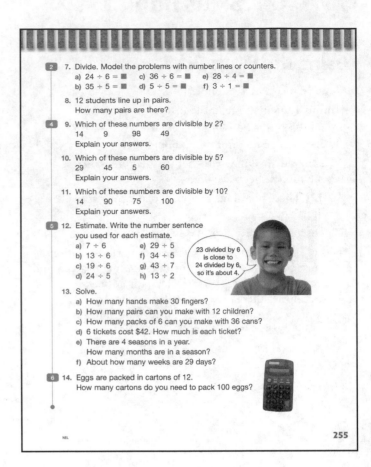

7. Divide. Model the problems with number lines or counters.
a) $24 \div 6 = \blacksquare$ c) $36 \div 6 = \blacksquare$ e) $28 \div 4 = \blacksquare$
b) $35 \div 5 = \blacksquare$ d) $5 \div 5 = \blacksquare$ f) $3 \div 1 = \blacksquare$

8. 12 students line up in pairs.
How many pairs are there?

9. Which of these numbers are divisible by 2?
14   9   98   49
Explain your answers.

10. Which of these numbers are divisible by 5?
29   45   5   60
Explain your answers.

11. Which of these numbers are divisible by 10?
14   90   75   100
Explain your answers.

12. Estimate. Write the number sentence you used for each estimate.
a) $7 \div 6$ e) $29 \div 5$
b) $13 \div 6$ f) $34 \div 5$
c) $19 \div 6$ g) $43 \div 7$
d) $24 \div 5$ h) $13 \div 2$

23 divided by 6 is close to 24 divided by 6, so it's about 4.

13. Solve.
a) How many hands make 30 fingers?
b) How many pairs can you make with 12 children?
c) How many packs of 6 can you make with 36 cans?
d) 6 tickets cost $42. How much is each ticket?
e) There are 4 seasons in a year.
How many months are in a season?
f) About how many weeks are 29 days?

14. Eggs are packed in cartons of 12.
How many cartons do you need to pack 100 eggs?

NEL

255

Problem Bank

Using the Problem Bank

Materials: counters, number lines, toothpicks

3. Writing the nine numbers on paper squares may be helpful for students.

Related Questions to Ask

Ask	Possible Response
About Question 1: • Can more than six children share the posters equally? How does your answer help narrow down the answers to Question 1?	• *Since there are only six posters, these cannot be shared by more than six students (unless they do so as teams).*
About Questions 2 and 5: • Both of these questions involve divisions that have some left over. For Question 2, the answer becomes one more than the quotient. For Question 5, the answer is just the quotient. Why the difference?	• *For Question 2, the cars have to hold all of the people. Another car has to be added to hold those left over from the division groupings. For Question 5, the cost of the bunches has to fit within the money given, so the quotient is not increased as in Question 2.*
About Question 6: • How can you start with the fact that Stella bought at least two of each kind of sticker?	• *Find the cost for these six stickers and subtract that cost from 30 cents.*

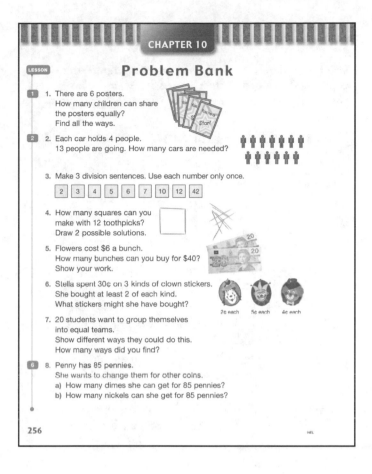

CHAPTER 10

LESSON

Problem Bank

1. 1. There are 6 posters.
   How many children can share the posters equally?
   Find all the ways.

2. 2. Each car holds 4 people.
   13 people are going. How many cars are needed?

3. Make 3 division sentences. Use each number only once.

   2 3 4 5 6 7 10 12 42

4. How many squares can you make with 12 toothpicks?
   Draw 2 possible solutions.

5. Flowers cost $6 a bunch.
   How many bunches can you buy for $40?
   Show your work.

6. Stella spent 30¢ on 3 kinds of clown stickers.
   She bought at least 2 of each kind.
   What stickers might she have bought?

   2¢ each   5¢ each   4¢ each

7. 20 students want to group themselves into equal teams.
   Show different ways they could do this.
   How many ways did you find?

6. 8. Penny has 85 pennies.
   She wants to change them for other coins.
   a) How many dimes she can get for 85 pennies?
   b) How many nickels can she get for 85 pennies?

256

Answers

1. There are 4 ways in all.
   $6 \div 6 = 1$ poster each for 6 students
   $6 \div 3 = 2$ posters each for 3 students
   $6 \div 2 = 3$ posters each for 2 students
   $6 \div 1 = 6$ posters each for 1 student

2. 4

3. There are 6 possibilities:
   $42 \div 6 = 7$ or $42 \div 7 = 6$
   $12 \div 3 = 4$ or $12 \div 4 = 3$
   $10 \div 2 = 5$ or $10 \div 5 = 2$

4. For example:
   3 squares:

4 squares, with some toothpicks forming the side of more than 1 square:

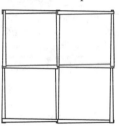

8 squares, with toothpicks allowed to cross:

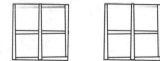

5. 6 bunches

6. six 2¢ stickers, two 5¢ stickers, two 4¢ stickers

7. 5 solutions are possible:
   1 team of 20
   2 teams of 10
   4 teams of 5
   5 teams of 4
   10 teams of 2

8. a) 8 dimes   **b)** 17 nickels

Chapter Review

Using the Chapter Review

Use these pages to assess students' understanding of the concepts developed in the chapter. Refer to the assessment chart on pages 45–46 for the details of each question.

Preparation and Planning

Materials	• counters
Workbook	p. 83, all questions
Masters	• Number Lines, Masters Booklet p. 34 • Chapter 10 Test Pages 1 & 2, pp. 52–53

2. Remind students to provide two solutions, using pictures, words, and number sentences.

3. Compare the methods used to solve this question and Question 11 a). Both can be represented as $25 \div 5 = 5$.

7. Before assigning this question, have the class read Questions 5 and 6 aloud and discuss.

9. Ask students having difficulty to list the numbers from 20 to 28. Each of these numbers can be tested for the divisors 2 and 5.

11. a) Compare the methods used to solve this question and Question 3. Both can be represented as $25 \div 5 = 5$.

Related Questions to Ask

Ask	Possible Response
About **Question 9:** • What numbers between 19 and 29 are divisible by 2? How can that help you to solve this problem? What is left to do?	• *20, 22, 24, 26, and 28, which all end in even digits. The house number has to be one of those. You still have to find which of those is divisible by 5.*

Journal

Ask students to record in their journals their thoughts, having now completed the chapter, about the chapter goal that they wrote about at the beginning of the chapter. (See Chapter Opener, Teacher's Resource p. 9.) Then have them compare their responses and reflect on what they have learned.

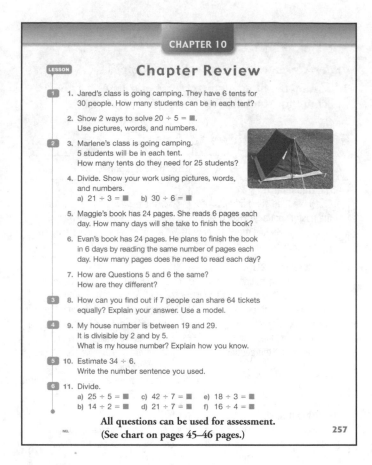

CHAPTER 10

LESSON

Chapter Review

1 1. Jared's class is going camping. They have 6 tents for 30 people. How many students can be in each tent?

2. Show 2 ways to solve $20 \div 5 = \blacksquare$. Use pictures, words, and numbers.

2 3. Marlene's class is going camping. 5 students will be in each tent. How many tents do they need for 25 students?

4. Divide. Show your work using pictures, words, and numbers.
   a) $21 \div 3 = \blacksquare$ b) $30 \div 6 = \blacksquare$

5. Maggie's book has 24 pages. She reads 6 pages each day. How many days will she take to finish the book?

6. Evan's book has 24 pages. He plans to finish the book in 6 days by reading the same number of pages each day. How many pages does he need to read each day?

7. How are Questions 5 and 6 the same? How are they different?

3 8. How can you find out if 7 people can share 64 tickets equally? Explain your answer. Use a model.

4 9. My house number is between 19 and 29. It is divisible by 2 and by 5. What is my house number? Explain how you know.

5 10. Estimate $34 \div 6$. Write the number sentence you used.

6 11. Divide.
   a) $25 \div 5 = \blacksquare$ c) $42 \div 7 = \blacksquare$ e) $18 \div 3 = \blacksquare$
   b) $14 \div 2 = \blacksquare$ d) $21 \div 7 = \blacksquare$ f) $16 \div 4 = \blacksquare$

All questions can be used for assessment.
(See chart on pages 45–46 pages.)

NEL   257

Answers

1. 5 students

2. 4 groups of 5 or 5 groups of 4

3. 5 tents

4. a) 7   **b)** 5

5. 4 days

6. 4 pages

7. Similarities: Both Questions 5 and 6 can be solved by dividing, using the division sentence $24 \div 6 = 4$. Both involve reading equal groups of pages in a book each day.

Differences: The answer to Question 5 is 4 days. The answer to Question 6 is 4 pages.

8. Seven people cannot share 64 tickets equally. For example, let a counter represent a ticket. There are 64 counters in all. I can make 7 piles with 9 in each pile. One counter is left over.

9. 20 is the house number. For example, the numbers between 19 and 29 that are divisible by 2 are 20, 22, 24, 26, and 28. The numbers between 19 and 29 that are divisible by 5 are 20 and 25. Only 20 is on both lists. For example, a number is divisible by 10 if it is divisible by 2 and 5. The only number between 19 and 29 divisible by 10 is 20.

10. about 6; $6 \times 6 = 36$

11. a) 5   **b)** 7   **c)** 6   **d)** 3   **e)** 6   **f)** 4

Assessment of Learning—What to Look for in Student Work...

Assessment Strategy: short answer
Understanding of Concepts

Question 1
• Jared's class is going camping. They have 6 tents for 30 people. How many students can be in each tent?
  (Score 1 point for the correct response.)

Assessment Strategy: written question
Communication

Question 2
• Show 2 ways to solve $20 \div 5 = \blacksquare$. Use pictures, words, and numbers.

1	2	3	4
• provides incomplete solutions using minimal pictures, words, and numbers	• provides partial solutions using some pictures, words, and numbers	• provides complete solutions using appropriate pictures, words, and numbers	• provides thorough solutions using a range of pictures, words, and numbers

---

Assessment Strategy: short answer
Understanding of Concepts

Question 3
• Marlene's class is going camping. 5 students will be in each tent. How many tents do they need for 25 students?
  (Score 1 point for the correct response.)

Assessment Strategy: written question
Communication

Question 4
• Divide. Show your work using pictures, words, and numbers.
  a) $21 \div 3 = \blacksquare$ **b)** $30 \div 6 = \blacksquare$

1	2	3	4
• provides incomplete solutions using minimal pictures, words, and numbers	• provides partial solutions using some pictures, words, and numbers	• provides complete solutions using appropriate pictures, words, and numbers	• provides thorough solutions using a range of pictures, words, and numbers

---

Assessment Strategy: short answer
Understanding of Concepts

Question 5
• Maggie's book has 24 pages. She reads 6 pages each day. How many days will she take to finish the book?
  (Score 1 point for the correct response.)

Assessment Strategy: short answer
Understanding of Concepts

Question 6
• Evan's book has 24 pages. He plans to finish the book in 6 days by reading the same number of pages each day. How many pages does he need to read each day?
  (Score 1 point for the correct response.)

Assessment Strategy: written question
Communication

Question 7
• How are Questions 5 and 6 the same? How are they different?

1	2	3	4
• provides an incomplete explanation that lacks clarity or logical thought	• provides a partial explanation that exhibits some clarity and logical thought	• provides a complete, clear, and logical explanation for how the two questions are the same and how they are different	• provides a thorough, clear, and insightful explanation for how the two questions are the same and how they are different
• uses very little mathematical language correctly	• uses some mathematical language correctly	• uses mathematical language correctly	• uses precise mathematical language

Assessment of Learning—What to Look for in Student Work...

Assessment Strategy: written question
Communication

Question 8

• How can you find out if 7 people can share 64 tickets equally? Explain your answer. Use a model.

1	2	3	4
• provides an incomplete explanation of the solution that lacks clarity or logical thought	• provides a partial explanation of the solution that exhibits some clarity and logical thought	• provides a complete, clear, and logical explanation of the solution	• provides a thorough, clear, and insightful explanation of the solution
• uses very little mathematical language correctly	• uses some mathematical language correctly	• uses mathematical language correctly	• uses precise mathematical language
• model used is inappropriate	• model used is partially appropriate	• model used is appropriate	• model used is appropriate

Assessment Strategy: written question
Problem Solving

Question 9

• My house number is between 19 and 29. It is divisible by 2 and 5. What is my house number? Explain how you know.

1	2	3	4
Make a Plan	**Make a Plan**	**Make a Plan**	**Make a Plan**
• little or no evidence of a plan	• evidence of a partial plan	• evidence of an appropriate plan	• evidence of a thorough plan
Carry Out the Plan	**Carry Out the Plan**	**Carry Out the Plan**	**Carry Out the Plan**
• uses a strategy to find the house number, but does not arrive at an answer	• carries out the plan to some extent using a strategy, and develops a partial and/or incorrect plan	• carries out the plan effectively to find the house number	• shows flexibility and insight by trying and adapting one or more strategies to find the house number
Communicate	**Communicate**	**Communicate**	**Communicate**
• provides an incomplete explanation of the solution that lacks clarity or logical thought	• provides a partial explanation of the solution that exhibits some clarity and logical thought	• provides a complete, clear, and logical explanation of the solution	• provides a thorough, clear, and insightful explanation of the solution
• uses very little mathematical language correctly	• uses some mathematical language correctly	• uses mathematical language correctly	• uses precise mathematical language

Assessment Strategy: written question
Problem Solving

Question 10

Estimate 34 ÷ 6. Write the number sentence you used.

1	2	3	4
Carry Out the Plan	**Carry Out the Plan**	**Carry Out the Plan**	**Carry Out the Plan**
• uses a strategy to estimate, but does not arrive at an answer	• carries out the plan to some extent using a strategy, and develops a partial and/or incorrect plan	• carries out the plan effectively by using a model and multiplication to estimate	• shows flexibility and insight by using a model and multiplication to estimate

Assessment Strategy: short answer
Application of Procedures

Question 11

• Divide.

   a) 25 ÷ 5 = ■   **c)** 42 ÷ 7 = ■   **e)** 18 ÷ 3 = ■
   b) 14 ÷ 2 = ■   **d)** 21 ÷ 7 = ■   **f)** 16 ÷ 4 = ■
   (Score correct responses out of 6.)

Chapter Task

Expectations

3m4 understand and explain basic operations (addition, subtraction, multiplication, division) involving whole numbers by modelling and discussing a variety of problem situations

3m7 select and perform computation techniques (addition, subtraction, multiplication, division) appropriate to specific problems, and determine whether the results are reasonable

3m27 demonstrate and recall multiplication facts to 7×7, and division facts to $49 \div 7$, using concrete materials

3m32 use appropriate strategies to solve number problems involving whole numbers

Use this task as an opportunity for performance assessment, to give you a sense of students' understanding and explanation of division, and their experience using strategies to solve division problems.

Preparation and Planning

Pacing	**10–20 min** Introducing the Chapter Task **30–40 min** Dividing a Recipe
Materials	• (optional) counters/tiles • (optional) student-made multiplication tables
Masters	• Chapter 10 Test Pages 1 & 2, pp 52–53
Enabling Activities	• Share to divide. (See Getting Started & Lesson 1.) • Group to divide. (See Lesson 2.) • Communicate about division. (See Lesson 3.)
Nelson Web Site	Visit **www.mathk8.nelson.com** and follow the links to *Nelson Mathematics 3*, Chapter 10, to view samples of students' work and assessment support notes.

CHAPTER 10

Chapter Task

Dividing a Recipe

Malik wants to make a batch of fruit punch to share with friends. If he follows the recipe, he will have too much punch.

Fruit Punch
12 cups of apple juice
16 cups of grape juice
8 cups of ginger ale

? **How can Malik make a smaller batch of punch?**

Part 1
A. Suppose Malik decides to divide the recipe by 2. How many cups of each ingredient will he need? Show your work. Check that you are right.

B. How many cups of punch will he make altogether? Show your work.

Part 2
C. Malik can divide the recipe another way instead of by 2. He still uses only whole cups of each ingredient. Show how he can do this. Check that you are right.

Task Checklist
☑ Did you show all your steps?
☑ Did you use math language?

258   NEL

Introducing the Chapter Task
(Whole Class) ▶ 10–20 min

- Brainstorm with the class types of recipes that can be shared with several people (e.g., a batch of cookies, punch, chili, rice, ravioli, etc.).
- Pose the problem, "If you were making a batch of cookies for 24 people, and the recipe only made enough for 12 people, what would you have to do to the recipe?" (Double each ingredient so you are making twice as much.)
- Pose another problem, "If you were making some chili for 10 people, but the recipe made enough for 30 people, what would you have to do to the recipe?" (Divide each ingredient by 3, so you are making only enough for 10 people.)
- Ask the class what you need to do to a recipe if you want to make it for more people. (Multiply each ingredient.) Ask the class what you need to do to a recipe if you want to make if for fewer people. (Divide each ingredient.)
- Review with the class that multiplication is repeated addition, and division is equal sharing or grouping. When you want to increase the size of something, like a recipe, use multiplication. When you want to decrease the size of a recipe, use division.

Using the Chapter Task
(Individual) ▶ 30–40 min

Read all the information on Student Book page 258 together. Point out that the Task Checklist shows reminders about how to achieve an excellent solution.

Some students may be able to work through the task as it is described on the student page; however, most will benefit from using the master to plan and record work. Students should be able to use whatever materials they need for support (e.g., counters, tiles, student-made multiplication tables).

Point out that Malik cannot make a smaller batch by just leaving out an ingredient. Rather, he must reduce the amount of each ingredient for the taste be the same.

Students should discover that Malik needs 6 cups of apple juice, 8 cups of grape juice, and 4 cups of ginger ale. Malik will have 18 cups of punch altogether.

For Part 2, the recipe can also be divided evenly by 4, so then Malik would have 3 cups of apple juice, 4 cups of grape juice, and 2 cups of ginger ale. Malik will have 9 cups of punch altogether.

While students are working, observe and/or interview individuals to see how they are interpreting and carrying out the task.

If you want to consider a different performance assessment idea, see Adapting the Task.

Assessing Student Work

Use the chart below as a guide for assessing students' work. To view samples of students' work at different levels, visit the Nelson Web site at **www.mathk8.nelson.com**.

Adapting the Task

You can adapt the task in the Student Book to suit the needs of your students. For example:
- Use Chapter 10 Task Pages 1 & 2, pp. 54–55.
- Allow students to complete Parts 1 and 2 orally, rather than in writing.
- Use different amounts of juice than the ones given in the original question.
- For an enrichment to the task and a connection to the previous chapter on multiplication, tell students that Malik needs twice as much fruit punch as the original recipe.
- To share his punch from Part 1 with 9 people (including Malik), how many cups will each person will get? (3)
- To share his punch from Part 2 with 9 people (including Malik), how many cups will each person will get? (1)

Assessment of Learning—What to Look for in Student Work...

Assessment Strategy: observation and product marking
Problem Solving

Category	1	2	3	4
Problem Solving **Prompts A, B, & C** Do: Carry Out the Plan	• uses a strategy and attempts to solve the problems (how many cups of each ingredient Malik will need, and how much punch he will make altogether), but does not arrive at an answer	• uses a strategy and develops a partial and/or incorrect solution to solve the problems (how many cups of each ingredient Malik will need, and how much punch he will make altogether)	• uses an appropriate strategy to solve the problems (how many cups of each ingredient Malik will need, and how much punch he will make altogether)	• shows flexibility and insight by trying one or more strategies to solve the problems (how many cups of each ingredient Malik will need, and how much punch he will make altogether)
Problem Solving **Prompts A & C** Look Back: Review Solution	• is unable to identify either errors or omissions in the attempted solution	• has some difficulty checking the attempted solution for errors and/or omissions	• checks the solution for procedural errors and omissions	• thoroughly reviews the solution for procedural errors and omissions to verify the answer and judge whether it is reasonable
Understanding of Concepts **Prompts A, B, & C** Depth of Understanding	• demonstrates a superficial or inaccurate understanding of division	• demonstrates a growing but still incomplete understanding of division	• demonstrates an appropriate understanding of division	• demonstrates an in-depth understanding of division
Application of Procedures **Prompts A, B, & C** Applying Procedures	• makes major errors and/or omissions when dividing and adding numbers	• makes several errors and/or omissions when dividing and adding numbers	• makes only a few minor errors and/or omissions when dividing and adding numbers	• makes almost no errors when dividing and adding numbers
Communication **Prompts A, B, & C** Organization of Material	• organization of the work is minimal and seriously impedes communication • steps followed are not shown	• organization of the work is limited but does not seriously impede communication • an attempt to show steps followed is made	• organization of the work is sufficient to support communication • all steps are shown	• organization of the work is effective and aids communication • all steps are shown

Family Newsletter

Dear Parent/Caregiver:

Over the next two weeks, your child will be learning about the concept of division. He or she will be learning division facts up to and including $49 \div 7$ and seeing the connection between multiplication and division and subtraction and division. The goal will be for your child to either recall division facts or be able to apply a strategy to find each answer. Your child will use these facts, along with a variety of strategies, to solve real-life problems.

Throughout this time, you and your child can do some activities such as:

- Your child can look for things that come in groups of 2s, 3s, and 4s (such as rolls of hockey tape, bags of milk, and so on).
- Your child can begin to calculate how to share things equally within a group of people. For example, if I had 12 stickers to share with 3 friends, how many stickers could we each have?
- Your child could find objects that come in arrays (such as muffins in a box or eggs in a carton). This would assist in connecting the multiplication and division fact families.

You may want to visit the Nelson Web site at **www.mathk8nelson.com** for more suggestions to help your child learn mathematics and develop a positive attitude toward learning mathematics, and for books that relate children's literature to multiplication and division. Also check the Web site for links to other sites that provide online tutorials, math problems, and brainteasers.

If your child is using the *Nelson Mathematics 3 Workbook*, pages 77 to 83 belong kto Chapter 10. There is a page of practice questions for each of the 6 lessons in the chapter and a Test Yourself page at the end. If your child requires assistance, you can refer to the At-Home Help box on each Workbook page.

Chapter 10 Mental Math Page 1

LESSON

1

1. Shapes that are the same represent the same number.
   Use mental math to find the number.

   a) ■ + ■ = 10 _____

   b) ▲ + ▲ = 14 _____

   c) ■ + ■ + ■ = 15 _____

   d) ● + ● + ● + ● = 16 _____

   e) ▬ + ▬ + ▬ + ▬ + ▬ = 10 _____

   f) ● + ● + ● + ● + ● + ● = 24 _____

2

2. Continue each number pattern.
   Put a ✓ beside each pattern that ends at 0.

   a) Start at 12. Subtract 2 each time. _____

   b) Start at 25. Subtract 5 each time. _____

   c) Start at 50. Subtract 10 each time. _____

   d) Start at 12. Subtract 3 each time. _____

   e) Start at 15. Subtract 2 each time. _____

   f) Start at 16. Subtract 3 each time. _____

3

3. a) Circle the numbers in the table that can be divided by 2.

   b) Shade the numbers that can be divided by 3.

   c) Put a square around numbers that can be divided by 4.

   d) Which numbers have been circled, shaded, and have a square
      around them?

1	2	3	4	5	6	7	8	9	10
11	12	13	14	15	16	17	18	19	20

Chapter 10 Mental Math Page 2

LESSON

4

4. Use mental math to solve each problem.

   a) You count 15 wheels. How many tricycles are there? _____

   b) You count 12 eyes. How many people are there? _____

   c) You count 18 legs. How many ants are there? _____

   d) You count 20 fingers. How many hands are there? _____

   e) You count 21 days. How many weeks are there? _____

5. Use the 1st division sentence to help you complete the 2nd one.

   a) $10 \div 2 = 5$ $100 \div 2 =$ _____

   b) $4 \div 2 = 2$ $40 \div 2 =$ _____

   c) $6 \div 3 = 2$ $60 \div 3 =$ _____

   d) $9 \div 3 = 3$ $90 \div 3 =$ _____

   e) $8 \div 4 = 2$ $80 \div 4 =$ _____

6. Use division to find each mystery number.

   a) When you divide me by 2, my answer is 6 with 1 left over. _____

   b) When you divide me by 3, my answer is 3 with 2 left over. _____

   c) When you divide me by 5, my answer is 2 with none left over. _____

   d) When you divide me by 6, my answer is 3 with 2 left over. _____

Chapter 10 Test Page 1

1. Jared's class is going boating.
   There are 4 boats for 24 students.
   How many students may be in each boat?
   Show your work.

2. Show 2 ways to solve $15 \div 3 = \blacksquare$.
   Use pictures, words, and numbers.

3. Marlene's class is going boating.
   8 students will be in each boat.
   How many boats will they need for 24 students?
   Show 2 ways to find the answer.
   You may use a number line, counters, pictures, words, and numbers.

   _____ ÷ _____ = _____

4. Divide.

   a) $15 \div 5 =$ _____   **b)** $18 \div 3 =$ _____

5. Maggie's magazine has 12 pages.
   She reads 3 pages each hour.
   How many hours will it take her to finish the magazine? _____

6. Maggie's magazine has 12 pages.
   She plans to finish the magazine in 3 hours.
   How many pages does she need to read each hour? _____

Chapter 10 Test Page 2

7. Can 6 people share 46 tickets equally?
Explain your answer.

8. There is a mystery number between 29 and 39.
It is divisible by both 2 and 5.

Write the number. _____
Explain how you know.

9. a) Estimate $27 \div 5$. _____

b) Write the number sentence you used.

_____ × _____ = _____

10. Divide.

a) $16 \div 4 =$ _____   **c)** $15 \div 5 =$ _____   **e)** $36 \div 6 =$ _____

b) $16 \div 2 =$ _____   **d)** $28 \div 7 =$ _____   **f)** $42 \div 6 =$ _____

11. Use a calculator to estimate $230 \div 8$ using either the multiplication or
division keys.

Chapter 10 Task Page 1

Dividing a Recipe

STUDENT BOOK PAGE 258

Malik wants to make a batch of fruit punch to share with friends.
If he follows the recipe, he will have too much punch.

Fruit Punch
12 cups of apple juice
16 cups of grape juice
8 cups of ginger ale

❓ How can Malik make a smaller batch of punch?

Read the Task Checklist before you begin.

Part 1

A. Suppose Malik decides to divide the recipe by 2.
How many cups of each ingredient will he need?
Show your work. Check that you are right.

B. How many cups of punch will he make altogether?
Show your work.

Chapter 10 Task Page 2

Part 2

C. Malik can divide the recipe another way instead of by 2.
He still uses only whole cups of each ingredient.
Show how he can do this.
Check that you are right.

Scaffolding for Getting Started Activity

STUDENT BOOK PAGES 238–239

A. 3 friends want to share 12 tickets equally.
Colour to show 12 tickets being shared by 3 friends.

How many tickets will each person get? _____

B. Keenan joins the group of 3 before they use any tickets.
Colour to show 12 tickets being shared by 4 friends.

How many tickets will each person get now? _____

C. Karla can get 3 cones of animal feed for 1 ticket.
Colour 1 ticket for every 3 cones.

How many tickets will she need for 15 cones? _____

D. Krista buys 9 tickets. A Zoomobile ride costs 3 tickets
for each rider. Colour 3 tickets for Krista.
Use a different colour. Colour 3 tickets for another rider.
Repeat until you run out of tickets.

How many friends can Krista can take with her? _____
How do you know?

Scaffolding for Do You Remember? Page 1

STUDENT BOOK PAGE 239

1. Write the next 3 numbers in each skip counting pattern.

a) 0, 2, 4, 6, 8, _____, _____, _____

b) 0, 5, 10, 15, 20, _____, _____, _____

2. Multiply.

a) $2 \times 7 =$ _____

2 groups of 7

b) $6 \times 3 =$ _____

6 groups of 3

c) $4 \times 5 =$ _____

4 groups of 5

d) $5 \times 3 =$ _____

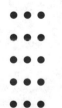

5 groups of 3

e) $2 \times 6 =$ _____

2 groups of 6

f) $1 \times 7 =$ _____

1 groups of 7

g) $5 \times 5 =$ _____

5 groups of 5

h) $7 \times 7 =$ _____

7 groups of 7

Name: _____ Date: _____

Scaffolding for Do You Remember? Page 2

3. Write the next 3 numbers in each skip-counting pattern.

   a) 35, 30, 25, 20, 15, _____, _____, _____

   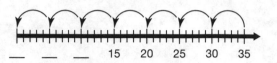

   b) 14, 12, 10, 8, 6, _____, _____, _____

   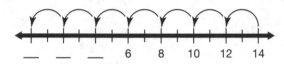

4. The pattern rule is "Start at 24 and subtract 4."

   a) Write the numbers in the pattern. Continue to 0.

   24, 20, _____, _____, _____, _____, _____,

   b) How many times did you subtract 4? _____

Scaffolding for Lesson 2, Questions 5–8
STUDENT BOOK PAGE 243

5. How many groups of 7 line dancers can you make? Model the groups with counters or number lines. Write a division sentence.

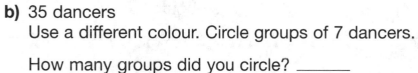

   a) 21 dancers
   Circle groups of 7 dancers.

   How many groups did you circle? _____

   There are _____ groups of 7 dancers in 21.

   b) 35 dancers
   Use a different colour. Circle groups of 7 dancers.

   How many groups did you circle? _____

   There are _____ groups of 7 dancers in 35.

6. Divide

   a) 20 ÷ 5 = _____   **c)** 21 ÷ 3 = _____   **e)** 28 ÷ 4 = _____

   b) 30 ÷ 6 = _____   **d)** 18 ÷ 6 = _____   **f)** 4 ÷ 1 = _____

7. Graham has 10 tickets.

   a) How many people can have 2 tickets each?

   b) How many people can have 3 tickets each?

8. This is a division sentence about dancers: 28 ÷ 4 = _____

   Create and solve a problem about the dancers.

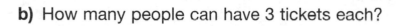

Scaffolding for Lesson 5, Questions 5–7

STUDENT BOOK PAGE 251

5. Estimate. Write the number sentence you used for each estimate.
For each division sentence, estimate the number of stars that would be
in each group. Circle the correct number of stars in each group.

a) $17 \div 5$

   $5 \times$ ____ = ____ $17 \div 5$ is about ____.

   ☆☆☆☆☆☆☆☆☆☆☆☆☆☆☆☆☆

b) $34 \div 5$

   $5 \times$ ____ = ____ $34 \div 5$ is about ____.

   ☆☆☆☆☆☆☆☆☆☆☆☆☆☆☆☆☆☆☆☆☆☆☆☆☆☆☆☆☆☆☆☆☆☆

c) $17 \div 6$

   $6 \times$ ____ = ____ $17 \div 6$ is about ____.

   ☆☆☆☆☆☆☆☆☆☆☆☆☆☆☆☆☆

d) $35 \div 6$

   $6 \times$ ____ = ____ $35 \div 6$ is about ____.

   ☆☆☆☆☆☆☆☆☆☆☆☆☆☆☆☆☆☆☆☆☆☆☆☆☆☆☆☆☆☆☆☆☆☆☆☆

e) $21 \div 6$

   $6 \times$ ____ = ____ $21 \div 6$ is about ____.

   ☆☆☆☆☆☆☆☆☆☆☆☆☆☆☆☆☆☆☆☆☆

f) $30 \div 4$

   $4 \times$ ____ = ____ $30 \div 4$ is about ____.

   ☆☆☆☆☆☆☆☆☆☆☆☆☆☆☆☆☆☆☆☆☆☆☆☆☆☆☆☆☆☆

6. Estimate. Explain each estimate.

   a) the number of weeks in a month with 31 days

   b) 20 pencils shared by 7 students

   c) $52 to buy 7 posters

7. 3 teachers share 25 posters.
About how many posters will each teacher get?

Scaffolding for Lesson 6, Questions 5–9

STUDENT BOOK PAGE 253

5. 3 tennis balls can be stacked in a container.
The tennis club collected 85 loose balls.
How many containers would 85 balls fill?
Use your calculator.

1st guess	Try 3 × 10 = _____.	This answer is too _____.
2nd guess	Try 3 × 20 = _____.	This answer is too _____.

Are you getting closer or further away from 85? _____

3rd guess	Try 3 × _____ = _____.	This answer is _____.
4th guess	Try 3 × _____ = _____.	This answer is _____.

85 balls would fill _____ containers.

6. 289 students need to divide themselves into 15 teams for play day.
How many students will be on each team?

7. A tall building has 168 steps. There are 12 steps between floors.
How many floors does the building have?

8. Jeff is 102 months old. How many years old is he?

9. Margaret's birthday is 100 days away.
How many weeks away is her birthday?

Beginning Division Strips (Math Game)

2	4	6	8	10	12	14	÷2
3	6	9	12	15	18	21	÷3
4	8	12	16	20	24	28	÷4
5	10	15	20	25	30	35	÷5
6	12	18	24	30	36	42	÷6
7	14	21	28	35	42	49	÷7

Mixed Division Strips (Math Game)

8	6	12	14	2	12	10	÷2
12	18	21	3	15	6	9	÷3
16	20	12	28	8	24	4	÷4
25	15	35	30	10	5	20	÷5
6	30	42	24	36	18	12	÷6
42	35	14	7	49	21	28	÷7

Number Cards (Math Game)

1	2	3	4	5	6	7
1	2	3	4	5	6	7
1	2	3	4	5	6	7
1	2	3	4	5	6	7
1	2	3	4	5	6	7
1	2	3	4	5	6	7
1	2	3	4	5	6	7
1	2	3	4	5	6	7

Chapter 10 Answers

Problem of the Week p. 3

1. 4

2. For example, use counters to represent tickets. Share 44 counters among 6 groups. Each group has 7. Two counters are left over.

Chapter 10 Mental Math pp. 50–51

1. **a)** 5   **b)** 7   **c)** 5   **d)** 4   **e)** 2   **f)** 4

2. **a)** 12, 10, 8, 6, 4, 2, 0 ✓

   b) 25, 20, 15, 10, 5, 0 ✓

   c) 50, 40, 30, 20, 10, 0 ✓

   d) 12, 9, 6, 3, 0 ✓

   e) 15, 13, 11, 9, 7, 5, 3, 1 ✗

   f) 16, 13, 10, 7, 4, 1 ✗

3. **a)** 2, 4, 6, 8, 10, 12, 14, 16, 18, 20

   b) 3, 6, 9, 12, 15, 18

   c) 4, 8, 12, 16, 20

   d) 12

4. **a)** 3   **b)** 6   **c)** 3   **d)** 4   **e)** 3

5. **a)** 50   **b)** 20   **c)** 20   **d)** 30   **e)** 20

6. **a)** 13   **b)** 11   **c)** 10   **d)** 20

Chapter 10 Test pp. 52–53

1. 6

2. For example: I have 15 counters and I start sharing them among 3 piles. When I finish sharing my counters, I count and see that there are 5 counters in each pile, so $15 \div 3 = 5$.

3. $24 \div 8 = 3$; for example: Skip counting by 8 backward from 24, I can make 3 skips to 0, and there are no more students left.

4. **a)** 3   **b)** 6

5. 4 hours

6. 4 pages

7. No. Explanations will vary. See the Communication Rubric (Tool 9), Masters Booklet p. 10.

8. 30; for example, the numbers between 29 and 39 that are divisible by 2 are 30, 32, 34, 36, and 38. The numbers between 29 and 39 that are divisible by 5 are 30 and 35. Only 30 is on both lists.

9. about 5; $5 \times 5 = 25$

10. **a)** 4   **b)** 8   **c)** 3   **d)** 4   **e)** 6   **f)** 7

11. The quotient is between 28 and 29.

Chapter 10 Task pp. 54–55

A. For example:

Half of the apple juice is 6 cups because $12 \div 2 = 6$.

Half of the grape juice is 8 cups because $16 \div 2 = 8$.

Half of the ginger ale is 4 cups because $8 \div 2 = 4$.

I know that I am right because when I add the 6 cups of apple juice to another 6 cups of apple juice, I get 12 cups, and that is the amount of apple juice in the recipe ($6 + 6 = 12$). When I add 8 cups of grape juice to another 8 cups, I get 16 cups of grape juice, and that is the amount in the recipe ($8 + 8 = 16$). When I add 4 cups of ginger ale to another 4 cups, I get 8 cups of ginger ale, and that is the amount in the recipe ($4 + 4 = 8$).

B. For example, he will make 18 cups of punch because 6 cups and 8 cups and 4 cups are 18 cups. 6 + 8 + 4 = 18. When Malik divides the recipe by two, he will get 18 cups of punch altogether.

C. For example, Malik can divide the recipe by four.

12 cups of apple juice divided by 4 is 3 cups because $12 \div 4 = 3$.

16 cups of grape juice divided by 4 is 4 cups because $16 \div 4 = 4$.

8 cups of ginger ale divided by 4 is 2 cups because $8 \div 4 = 2$.

When I add them together, I get 9 cups because $3 + 4 + 2 = 9$.

I know that I am right because when I multiply 3 cups of apple juice by 4, it is 12 cups ($3 \times 4 = 12$), and that is the amount of apple juice in the recipe. When I multiply 4 cups of grape juice by 4, it is 16 cups ($4 \times 4 = 16$), and that is the amount of grape juice in the recipe. When I multiply 2 cups of ginger ale by 4, it is 8 cups ($2 \times 4 = 8$), and that is the amount of ginger ale in the recipe. Malik can divide the recipe by 4 and he will get 9 cups of punch altogether.

Scaffolding for Getting Started Activity p. 56

A. 4

B. 3

C. 5

D. 2. For example, Krista wants to go herself, so that takes 3 tickets. She has 6 tickets left— enough for 2 friends.

Scaffolding for Do You Remember? pp. 57–58

1. a) 10, 12, 14   **b)** 25, 30, 35

2. a) 14   **b)** 18   **c)** 20   **d)** 15   **e)** 12   **f)** 7   **g)** 25   **h)** 49

3. a) 10, 5, 0   **b)** 4, 2, 0

4. a) 24, 20, 16, 12, 8, 4, 0   **b)** 6 times

Scaffolding for Lesson 2 p. 59

5. a) There are 3 groups of dancers in 21.

    b) There are 5 groups of dancers in 35.

6. a) 4   **b)** 5   **c)** 7   **d)** 3   **e)** 7   **f)** 4

7. a) 5   **b)** 3

8. For example, 28 dancers are going to the festival. 4 dancers can ride in each car. How many cars do they need?

Scaffolding for Lesson 5 p. 60

5. a) For example, $5 \times 3 = 15$; $17 \div 5$ is about 3

    b) For example, $5 \times 7 = 35$; $34 \div 5$ is about 7

    c) For example, $6 \times 3 = 18$; $21 \div 6$ is about 3

    d) For example, $6 \times 6 = 36$; $35 \div 6$ is about 6

    e) For example, $6 \times 3 = 18$; $21 \div 6$ is about 3

    f) For example, $4 \times 7 = 28$; $30 \div 4$ is about 7

6. a) For example, there are 7 days in a week. 3 weeks would be 21 days (too low); 4 weeks would be 28 days (still low, but close); 5 weeks would be 35 days (too high). I estimate about 4 weeks.

    b) For example, I know that $7 \times 3 = 21$, and that is really close to 20. So I estimate that each child will get about 3 pencils.

    c) For example, I used a number line and started skip counting by 7. I was able to skip count 7 times before I got past 52. I estimate that a poster costs about $7.

7. about 8

Scaffolding for Lesson 6 p. 61

5.

1st guess	Try 3 × 10 = 30.	This answer is too low.
2nd guess	Try 3 × 20 = 60.	This answer is too low.
3rd guess	Try 3 × 30 = 90.	This answer is high.
4th guess	Try 3 × 29 = 87.	This answer is high.
5th guess	Try 3 × 28 = 84.	This answer is low.

85 balls will fill 28 containers.

6. For example, each team will have 19 students. There will be 4 left over.

7. 14

8. 8 years old

9. 14 weeks

Lesson 2 Answers (continued from p. 19)

5. **a)** 3; for example:

3 groups

21 ÷ 7 = 3

3 skips

21 ÷ 7 = 3

b) 5; for example:

5 groups

35 ÷ 7 = 5

5 skips

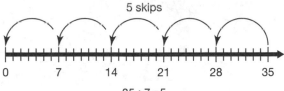

35 ÷ 7 = 5

6. **a)** 4   **b)** 5   **c)** 7   **d)** 3   **e)** 7   **f)** 4

7. **a)** 5   **b)** 3

8. For example, how many groups of 4 can you make with 28 dancers?
   (24 ÷ 4 = 7, so you can make 7 groups of 4 dancers.)

Lesson 4 Answers (continued from p. 30)

B. For example:

Nicola's pattern

1	2	3	4	5	6	7	8	9	10
11	12	13	14	15	16	17	18	19	20
21	22	23	24	25	26	27	28	29	30
31	32	33	34	35	36	37	38	39	40
41	42	43	44	45	46	47	48	49	50
51	52	53	54	55	56	57	58	59	60
61	62	63	64	65	66	67	68	69	70
71	72	73	74	75	76	77	78	79	80
81	82	83	84	85	86	87	88	89	90
91	92	93	94	95	96	97	98	99	100

Robin's pattern

1	2	3	4	5	6	7	8	9	10
11	12	13	14	15	16	17	18	19	20
21	22	23	24	25	26	27	28	29	30
31	32	33	34	35	36	37	38	39	40
41	42	43	44	45	46	47	48	49	50
51	52	53	54	55	56	57	58	59	60
61	62	63	64	65	66	67	68	69	70
71	72	73	74	75	76	77	78	79	80
81	82	83	84	85	86	87	88	89	90
91	92	93	94	95	96	97	98	99	100

Mo's pattern

1	2	3	4	5	6	7	8	9	10
11	12	13	14	15	16	17	18	19	20
21	22	23	24	25	26	27	28	29	30
31	32	33	34	35	36	37	38	39	40
41	42	43	44	45	46	47	48	49	50
51	52	53	54	55	56	57	58	59	60
61	62	63	64	65	66	67	68	69	70
71	72	73	74	75	76	77	78	79	80
81	82	83	84	85	86	87	88	89	90
91	92	93	94	95	96	97	98	99	100

C. For example, Nicola's pattern is a vertical line in the tens column. Robin's pattern is two vertical lines covering the top part of the tens column and the top part of the 5s column. Mo's pattern covers the top part of all the even-numbered columns.

D. For example, all of Nicola's numbers have 0 in the ones place.

E. For example, Nicola's numbers are all divisible by 2, and so are Mo's. All of the numbers in Mo's first column have 2 in the ones place. In the next column they have 4 in the ones place, then 6, then 8, then 10. All of Mo's numbers are even.

F. For example, Nicola's numbers are all divisible by 5, and so are Robin's. All of these numbers have 0 or 5 in the ones place.

1. 30 and 80. For example, they are both in the tens column on the 100 chart. It looks like all numbers on the 100 chart that have 0 in the ones place are divisible by 10.

2. For example, divisible by both 2 and 5: 10, 20, 30, 80
For example, divisible by 2 and not by 5: 16, 38, 42